THE GOOD MANAGER

THE GOOD MANAGER

A Guide for the
Twenty-First Century Manager

Dean Gualco

iUniverse, Inc.
New York   Bloomington

The Good Manager
A Guide for the Twenty-First Century Manager

iUniverse books may be ordered through booksellers or by contacting:

iUniverse
1663 Liberty Drive
Bloomington, IN 47403
www.iuniverse.com
1-800-Authors (1-800-288-4677)

Because of the dynamic nature of the Internet, any Web addresses or links contained in this book may have changed since publication and may no longer be valid.

ISBN: 978-1-4502-0657-0 (sc)
ISBN: 978-1-4502-0659-4 (dj)
ISBN: 978-1-4502-0658-7 (ebk)

Printed in the United States of America

iUniverse rev. date: 1/14/2010

Books by Dean Gualco:

What Happened to the American Dream (1995)

The Meaning of Life (2005)

The Great People of Our Time (2008)

To my children, Gunner and Toria,

who have given me a blessed life.

Always look for the good along the road of life.

Contents

Acknowledgments

I would like to extend my gratitude and appreciation to the following people, without whose contributions I would not be the man I am today.

- "The Man Upstairs," who has made this all possible.

- My parents, maternal grandmother (Vee McCoy), and paternal grandparents (Bocci and Rose Gualco), who gave me a great reputation to live up to.

- Keith Williams. Once or twice you make a friend that lasts a lifetime. For almost thirty years, Keith has been one of those friends, and I have been blessed.

- John Ellis. John and his wife Rachel just had their second child, and shortly thereafter he went to serve his country as a Marine in Afghanistan (for the third time!). There are few people I admire more than those in the military, not only for what they do for their country but the way they live their life.

- Bill Munroe. The personification of a good man trying to do good things with his time on Earth. He sets an extraordinary example for his children. In hoc, brother!

- Sierra Brucia. Simply a great guy who contributed his thoughts and ideas to this book, believing I had something important to contribute. Go Colts!

- John Solheim. Someone who lives a decent and honorable life. We should all be so fortunate.

- Jeff Thompson. A huge thank you to Jeff, his wife and kids for all they do to make my journey through life better. And thanks for the great help on this book.

Introduction

In the years following the end of World War II—a point at which the United States was at its zenith in terms of industrial and manufacturing dominance—managers were held in high regard and esteem by those in the political, economic, and social circles of our country. Employees felt a sense of trust in their managers and managers a sense of duty to their employees. That feeling has largely dissipated. An increasing number of books, magazine articles, and newspaper columns have been written denigrating the managerial profession and blaming the average manager for the distrust in our political institutions, the collapse of our economic system, and the stresses in our social compositions. This is not a fair assessment, and it is not accurate perception.

The field of management itself is a dynamic, exciting, and invigorating profession. It is also time consuming, stressful, and requires a constant retooling of an individual's knowledge and skills. It is far from a static, pedestrian profession. This is what makes the job of a manager so enticing, yet so intimidating. Given how challenging the profession often seems, it may be difficult for some to appreciate that being a good manager ultimately boils down to six simple, common attributes. The problem is determining those six common attributes and then remembering to display those attributes while meeting the often chaotic demands of a being a manager.

Based on my research of management and my experience as a manager, I propose the following six key attributes that a person should possess in order to master the art of management and to be generally viewed as a good, capable, decent, and honorable manager:

- **Like What You Do.** Good managers choose a job they like in a company they enjoy working for. It's difficult to be good at something if you don't enjoy doing it.

- **Knowledge.** The accumulation and utilization of knowledge is a defining characteristic of a good manager. Why? Without such knowledge it would be nearly impossible to excel at a central responsibility of a manager: to make the right decision at the right time and for the right reason. Managers know their job, their company, and their industry. They understand the mission and culture of their organization, and they are well educated and informed about the future of their industry.

- **Exceptional organizational skills.** Good managers perform a wide variety of duties and responsibilities, and in order to meet those expectations, they need three, broad organizational skills: the ability to plan, the ability to delegate, and the ability to manage time.

- **Work hard.** Nearly any "superstar" you meet in life—those who achieve spectacular success and achieve their phenomenal ambitions—possess great talent in their field, but then they work hard to perfect that talent. Good managers have this drive and determination and are willing to sacrifice.

- **Make Work Fun.** Fun is a basic human emotion and need, which is why some choose to travel, some play tennis, some read, and others go into business with their friends. We want to have fun because it enriches our souls and enlivens our spirits. Managers who sincerely care about people work to find the right person for the right job and have an extraordinary attitude to create a work environment where differing ideas are cherished and honest efforts rewarded. They create a fun place to work.

- **A Good Person.** An inability to control your insecurities, more than any other attribute, destroys the talents and promise of a manager. These insecurities are manifested in feelings of envy, jealously, greed, selfishness, contempt, and hate. Managers who possess the most comprehensive and developed combination of knowledge and skills, coupled with the greatest breadth and depth of education and experience, will fail utterly as managers (and as persons) unless they overcome these insecurities.

The writer Phillip Massinger believed: "He that would govern others, first should be the master of himself." If you want employees to be decent and honorable, you must first be decent and honorable. If you want your employees to do the right thing at the right time, you must first do the right thing at the right time. And if you want your employees to do and to be good, you must first do and be good yourself. Goodness is rarely learned at a conference you attend, or at a lecture you hear, or in a book you read. It is learned by those who are committed to helping their fellow man and advancing the interests of our world. It is, indeed, an incredibly high standard.

I truly believe those in the managerial profession endeavor to do their best and try to live an admirable life. Most are not in jail, they pay their taxes, and they generally make good decisions for their fellow employees and customers. We, unfortunately, rarely hear of these people in the news. Why? Because goodness does not sell, whereas treachery does. The people who manage their departments effectively, spend their incomes efficiently, control their expenses prudently, and are responsive to their clients and customers are rarely heard of. The person who mismanages the organization's financial resources, who takes advantage of his clients or customers, or who is lax or irresponsible in his duties or responsibilities—if it is to a great degree—has a chance of becoming infamous for their transgressions. He then becomes a symbol of everyone in their profession. The public, for some reason, is intrigued and interested in evil but raises little interest in goodness.

So, how does a good person, or a good manager, become bad? Is it a lack of knowledge or skills or consciousness or morals? Certainly those traits are absent—or in short supply—for bad people and bad managers. Rather than devoting efforts to determining why someone becomes bad, a better approach is to determine how a person can become good and how a manager with the requisite knowledge and moral clarity can learn to become a better manager and a better person. I am convinced that it can be done. All that is needed is a guide—someone to shine the light towards a better future, a future that is attainable through the sheer will and hard work of those who want a more fulfilling, peaceful, decent, and honorable future as a manager.

This book is intended to serve as that guide for future managers who aspire to join this vocation, for current managers who struggle to meet the often conflicting and confusing demands of their profession, and for employees who seek a better understanding and appreciation for the role of a manager in their organization. Ideally, this book illuminates a better future for managers as professionals and as people as well—people who can move along the intellectual and moral spectrum from self-interest to human interest, from negativity to positivity, from darkness to enlightenment, from hate to friendship, and from evil to good. Hopefully, after reading this book, there will be at least one more good manager added to our world.

The Changing Profession

The collapse of our economy has had a profound impact on the economic, political, and social fabric of our nation. Following catastrophic events of this nature, there is a natural tendency to find someone or something to blame, and two entities have received the most attention: the federal government and the managerial profession. The inability of government to accurately forecast and prevent this collapse has been well chronicled in a host of books and articles. Similarly, the mistakes by management to competently manage its business have grabbed the nation's attention, provoking anger at some manager's unethical and duplicitous conduct. This anger has been aimed at the managerial profession at large rather than to a minute segment of the profession that acted irresponsibly and unprofessionally.

I am convinced, though, that the image and profession of a manager can be rehabilitated. Identifying the attributes of a good manager, as outlined in this book, is an important contribution to that effort. First, however, it is beneficial to provide a broad context on the role of the manager in organizations along with how the circumstances and events of the past few years have fundamentally altered the profession, thus requiring a new way of thinking from today's manager.

THE MANAGER

"Manager" is a difficult term to define in business. This seems odd to some, especially since thousands of books have been written on the art and science of management, not including the countless books written about organizations, governments, and businesses, all in which a manager plays a key role in their success and failure. Yet, it is surprising how few managers can give a succinct and refined definition of management or understand the principal tenants of the managerial profession.

Let's start with a fairly basic definition of a manager: a manager is someone who has the responsibility to utilize an organization's material resources and to leverage cooperation from employees in order to attain a goal that is deemed important to the organization's success. What are these resources? Resources primarily revolve around people, money, and property; examples would include employees, computers, budgets, office space, volunteers, etc. Managers hope to utilize these resources in the most efficient and effective manner. By doing so they give the organization to which they belong a better chance of achieving its stated strategic objectives, whether that is producing a product or generating a service.

It is a common misunderstanding of the management profession to believe that managers and leaders are one and the same and that a good manager is also a good leader. A person can be both: some individuals can envision the future of an organization (a key trait of a leader) and then marshal the necessarily organizational resources to achieve that vision (a key role of a manager). I believe, though, that that distinction is more the exception than the rule. Each organizational role, both leader and a manager, has a different skill set, and it is the rare person who possesses both. Steve Jobs is a good example. Steve Jobs was the chief executive of Apple Computers for a number of years after its founding. He parted with the company a few years after its founding, having found that managing an organization is much different, and less interesting, than creating it. Of course, he later made a triumphant return to the top position at Apple Computers, having learned the skills necessary to manage an organization. His recent tenure at Apple Computers is a testament that managerial skills can be learned, if you have the knowledge, desire, and ability to do so.

A few more words need to be said about the distinction between a manager and a leader. Generally speaking, leaders set the overall direction of an organization. They determine the goals that the organization will pursue, and then they select the manager to achieve those goals. Managers, in contrast, have some influence on the direction of the organization but more so on how those goals are achieved. An analogy helps highlight the different roles a leader and a manager play in an organization. As a leader, you would determine the country to visit; as a manager, you would determine the best mode of transportation to get there and where to stay once you were there.

Successful organizations are created by visionary people with an idea or concept for something different and better. This success forces the organization to grow in size and scope; at this point, it often becomes necessary to hire a professional manager as the knowledge and skills necessary to create an organization are different than the knowledge and skills necessary to manage an organization. Leaders and managers both play vital roles in the organization, making it necessary that they possess the required knowledge, skills, and abilities that are unique to their profession, along with an understanding of the economic, political, and social events of the day. And rarely have events so tested the skills and abilities of managers as those occurring since 2008.

A COLLAPSE

Our nation's diminishing respect and confidence in management has been several years coming. We see employees who have lost their jobs, shareholders who have lost their investments, and homeowners who have lost their homes. Trillions of dollars have vanished in the stock market, and we are told that it may take years for the average American to recoup the investment in their home and retirement funds. Entire industries have been outsourced to foreign countries, along with the chance to obtain a solid middle-class job—one with a retirement plan and health benefits—that now seems out of reach for the average American. In fact, the middle-class job has become a faded relic of the past with unemployment hovering at numbers unseen since the last 1970s.

Not many have been immune from this economic reversal that started in 2008. Whether the fault of the federal government or much broader economic forces that have been in effect for decades, there has been a dramatic reversal of the American economy that began in 2008. Yet, somehow, the compensation of managers continues to increase. These often contradictory movements have caused stresses in our political, economic, and social systems, and they have contributed to the negative public perception of managers and their organizations that arose most prominently following the economic collapse in late 2008.

THE BLAME GAME

In this period of great uncertainty and instability, there is something quite American in looking for someone, anyone, to blame for our own and our nation's plight. Should we blame the thousands of real-estate agents and mortgage brokers who sold and financed homes to people who could not afford them? Should we blame the government, which failed to properly oversee the financial markets over the past decade? Should we blame the banks and financial institutions, which developed and promoted high-risk financial instruments that some believe were doomed to fail? Or should we blame those who manage our nation's businesses for their inability to act in a wise and prudent manner? In truth, all deserve some part of the blame. But there is merit to the assertion that at least some blame rests with a most uncomfortable segment of the population: us!

We've heard about the person who lost his home and blames the increase on his adjustable mortgage rate. On further investigation, we find out that the person never had the financial capability to purchase that home in the first place and instead was speculating that the home would go up in value, at which time he could then sell his home for a profit (preferably before interest rates rose and he could no longer afford his monthly payment). We've also heard of individuals who continually borrowed against their home to purchase a new car or build a pool in the backyard; then, when their house not only stopped increasing in value but actually decreased, they found themselves owing more for the house than it was worth. Some facing this situation have chosen to walk away from their financial obligations rather than accept responsibility for their actions and decisions and make good on their contract and word.

There was a segment of the population only too willing to enter into financial transactions without the knowledge necessary to make a competent decision. Some, it may be said, were greedy in accepting the benefits that the financial tools offered (for instance, buying a new home without any down payment or utilizing an adjustable rate mortgage to keep monthly mortgage loan costs down). Greed is not limited to those who tempted the average American to live beyond their means; it was also greedy for average Americans to believe they could enjoy a standard of living beyond their financial abilities to support it.

Some believe their fate would have been different had it not been for some unscrupulous person who took advantage of them and their lack of knowledge or sophistication in understanding the financial transaction that they were undertaking. There are the real-estate agents, mortgage brokers, and financial managers who preyed on a certain segment of the market, principally by creating financial transactions and mechanisms that the average person may not understand and therefore may not have the full knowledge about the actions that they were taking. These predators deserve to be prosecuted and made to pay for their deception. Moreover, some financial institutions and even governmental agencies encouraged the public to spend without saving and to extend financial obligations without prudent reserves, all because the economy appeared to be stable and financially sound. While that may be an optimistic attitude to have, it is not realistic, and the consequences of that optimistic, unrealistic attitude will affect the future of many Americans for years to come.

To be fair, some followed the advice and counsel of those paid to provide fair and honest advice (mortgage brokers, real-estate agents, and others). That said, however, too many borrowed more money than they could repay; too many entered into investments they could not afford; and too many simply lived beyond their means. The financial catastrophe of 2008–2009 rocked the foundation of many families mainly because so few were prepared for the financial correction or contraction that was bound to occur after a period of great economic growth. For many Americans with credit extended far beyond their means and savings too limited to maintain their lifestyle, the strains of our financial systems turned into a collapse, especially for those who were ill-prepared for any downturn in the economy.

We are partly to blame for the financial uncertainty that has become part of our lives. In previous times, we learned that Americans were savers, that they invested part of what they earned, that they believed in a solid work ethic, mutual responsibility, and taking some blame for bad decisions. We were taught to look inward if a mistake was made in order to find where the fault should lie.

Today, though, we tend to look outward first to assign blame and then cast ourselves as the unknowing and unwitting victims of some sort of predator. Indeed, we hear very little about the consequences of our own actions that have caused our financial hardships and instead read incessantly about the handful of individuals who created and promoted these destructive financial instruments that have wreaked havoc in our economy. Many Americans blame corporate managers, whether the CEO of the American Insurance Group (AIG) or the former CEO of General Motors, whose organizations profited from unethical financial transactions. In financial institutions, insurance companies, and the automakers, there is certainly a public face that you can find to blame for the cataclysmic fall of the many companies in these industries, regardless if that blame is justified. No matter who is to blame, there has risen a level of distrust and disgust about the ability and conduct of managers in some organizations, which has been extrapolated to all of corporate America.

Undoubtedly, there were a number of greedy, unscrupulous, and immoral people who were in a position to create great destruction within entire industries and to a wide segment of the American populace. Bad people do bad things; in this case, there were bad managers who adversely affected the fate of numerous organizations, employees, and investors, paralyzing the future of not only many in the business world but the whole of society as well.

These bad managers did not possess the moral and intellectual honesty, in addition to competence, to be stewards of their organization's future. They were impediments to organizations that wanted to take care of the customer, to grow the business reasonably, to create and sustain a quality product or service, and to make a reasonable profit. Profit, contrary to some thought, is not a negative consequence of the American business enterprise, but rather, it is a positive outcome of a person's or organization's honest effort to provide a quality product or service to a customer at a fair price.

An honest effort and fairness are the key tenants of a business, and it falls to managers to have the moral compass and fortitude to be honest and fair and to ensure that their conduct follows certain principles and practices. Not all managers are unscrupulous and immoral, just a select few, but it is those unfortunate few that have brought such damage and devastation to our economy. It is these select few that have tarnished the name and reputation of others in the managerial profession.

THE IMAGE OF A MANAGER

The action of a few managers has tarnished the name and reputation of others in the managerial profession; consequently, organizational managers struggle with a public perception that continues to go down hill. Besides the actions of a few managers that have contributed to the recent economic crisis, there are several other reasons to account for the misperception of managers by the public, with the most important being that managers tend to be blamed for most problems that occur in the organization. If employees are not meeting their goals, there are those who will say their manager is not providing the necessary guidance and support for the employees to excel. If the organization does not meet its goals, blame is typically assigned to management which, to be fair, is charged with the overall direction of the organization.

The second reason that management is not held in high esteem by the general public is because the manager must deliver the bad news to an employee. For example, if an employee is not given a promotion or raise, it is typically the manager who must relate this to the employee. If the employee is given more work, including work that had previously been done by the manager, the employee may feel the manager is not pulling his weight without regard to the added duties and responsibilities that may have necessitated the manager delegating this work to a subordinate. Of course, if any employee is disciplined, up to an including termination, that unfortunate news is typically delivered by the manager.

Third, managers tend to receive greater compensation than nonmanagers, which can be a source of tremendous jealously and envy within the organization. Few nonmanagers who I know believe the compensation managers receive is fair, and instead think such compensation should be more equitably distributed throughout the organization. On the other hand, I know very few nonmanagers who, once they were promoted, would say that their new manager salary is too high and the money should instead be distributed more equitably among staff.

Finally, some employees tend to view a manager's job as less demanding than their own. This thought arises because employees tend to do the more physical work whereas managers tend to do the mental or office-related work. A misperception may arise that the effort of a manager is not as pronounced as a no manager's, but there are certainly more demanding mental stresses within the managerial profession than in nonmanagerial jobs.

A REWARDING PROFESSION

Management is a truly rewarding profession. I know of very few people who willingly turn down a managerial position once offered; instead, those people tend to be dismissive of the profession mainly because they have not as yet joined its ranks or have determined that they may never be offered such opportunities in the future. In either case, their perceptions and beliefs about management may result more from jealously or envy than from the actual consequences of a managerial action. That is unfortunate and, to some, unfair.

For the vast majority of those in management, it is a fascinating profession full of financial and emotional rewards. There are six rewards, both personally and professionally, for those in the managerial profession. The first reward is money. Managers, in just about any profession and any organization, make more money that those not in management. This amount may be considerable. In some professions, a manager can make 20 percent to 40 percent more than nonmanagers, to the tune of tens or even hundreds of millions of dollars.

Some nonmanagers point to that salary differential as excessive or unfair, but they often fail to remember what a person needs to do in order to reap those financial rewards. For instance, those individuals promoted to management often had the most experience, the most appropriate education, and the best performance of anyone applying for the job. There are always exceptions, of course, of the less qualified promoted over the most qualified, but I believe that those are the exceptions rather than the rule. It would be a fair statement that those who have had the best performance are typically those promoted to higher positions, and with promotions come the higher salaries.

The second reward of management is greater freedom and control. Managers typically have greater freedom and control over their work and workplace than nonmanagers. For those who prefer to feel a sense of control over their lives, being a manager is one way to make that more likely. You have a greater opportunity to determine the work that you do and how you do it, and this greater latitude and discretion can lead to a more creative and exciting environment for the manager. For some, this offers a deeper sense of satisfaction in their jobs and greater enjoyment in their professions.

Here's an example: typically, managers are given a task or responsibility and then are encouraged to figure out the best way to accomplish that task. I once read a quote by General George S. Patton, who stated you should, "never tell someone how to do something; tell them what you want and they will surprise you with their ingenuity." Many in the management field enjoy this latitude, which also includes more autonomy in determining their own work schedules and duties.

A third reward for managers is they have more input into the direction of the organization. Organizations typically share more information with their managers than they do with nonmanagers. Some of this information is confidential: for instance, the focus of business or upcoming products or services. It would make sense that organizations share this information with managers and not the general public because the organizations would not want their competition to be forewarned as to their competitive strategies. Additionally, the managers will be responsible for implementing any new changes in the workplace, such as producing new products or services, so their input early in the process would be seen as important.

Allowing managers to provide input into the direction in which the organization is headed can give them a sense of importance. It also allows them to feel as if they are really contributing to the success of the organization and that their opinions and efforts may truly matter on the successful attainment of a goal. They also have at least some opportunity to voice their opinions and beliefs. For some, that is an incredible motivation in the workplace. One reason the use of groups and teams has been so successful is because they have allowed the ordinary individual to contribute to a greater extent.

Given that managers typically have more discretion in their duties and input into the future of their organization, a fourth reward for managers is that their circle of contacts or associates is significantly broader than nonmanagers. As a non-management employee, you typically have contact only with a supervisor and your coworkers. As a manager, your circle of associates is broader and grows to include subordinates, coworkers, and superiors. You have greater access to senior management, which again widens your circle of contacts and, hopefully, your circle of influence. Moreover, supervisors are typically more involved in workplace committees and group events, which again broadens your social network. For those who enjoy interaction with their fellow human beings, there are few better opportunities that allow you to interact with such a wide swath of individuals than being a manager.

The fifth reward of management is the opportunity and ability to help others in their lives. As a manager, you serve as a guide, mentor, and teacher to others. Whether it is improving their knowledge, skills, or abilities or some other form of help, it is a fantastic chance to change the professional and even personal life of someone you meet along your path. An example could be a sales manager who teaches his sales assistants the techniques to better sell a product or service or a finance manager who guides her trainees on how to review and audit a complex financial statement. The knowledge and experience that a manager can transmit to others certainly benefits the subordinate; most importantly, however, it is the sense of satisfaction that the manager receives from helping his fellow man or woman that is long remembered after the task is completed. At the end of a career, people tend to remember those who helped them along the way, and those, in turn, they helped along their path. It is a reward that some forget until late in their lives when they look back to determine their successes and failures. Their successes, inevitably, are centered on the people they knew and the kindness and assistance that were offered to them.

The sixth, and final, reward of being a manager is that the profession allows you the opportunity to transition into a new job with new responsibilities. Individuals promoted into the supervisory or managerial ranks often have to learn a new job and obtain new skills to be successful. What made an individual successful as a subordinate may not make them successful as a superior, so the learning of these new techniques, skills, and knowledge can be a motivating factor in their life.

There are few jobs that allow a person to grow both as an employee and as a person if they continue to do the same duties and responsibilities. As managers move through the organization, they perform a wider variety of duties and responsibilities. Task variety coupled with new and exciting challenges can raise an employee's interest and enthusiasm in his or her job, forestalling a sense of boredom and dissatisfaction that could arise if an employee remains in the same job performing similar tasks for an extended period of time.

SUMMARY: THE CHANGING PROFESSION

In the past few years, there has been a profound shift in the economic, political, and social foundations of our nation. Economically, the "Great Recession" has erased trillions of dollars in business and household wealth, at times calling into the question the stability of our capitalistic system. Politically, we've elected the nation's first African-American president, which brought along with it a sweeping change in political philosophy from conservative to a more liberal ideology. Socially, the prospect for the average citizen to obtain the American Dream—one in which the standard of living advances from generation to generation—

seems out of reach, with the middle-class job becoming a relic of the past.

During these challenging times, our society has searched for someone, anyone, to blame. Business has blamed government, and vice versa. Democrats have blamed Republications, and vice versa. The poor have blamed the rich, and vice versa. And, employees have blamed managers, and vice versa. In truth, all deserve to shoulder some blame for the perilous times we live in. Some in business created financial instruments that were ruinous to others; some in government were lax in regulation and oversight; some Democrats and Republications were engaged more in grandstanding and political expediency than in summoning the political will to address the serious problems of this nation; some employees failed to advance their skills to remain competitive in a changing workplace; and some managers were ill prepared and ill tempered to competently manage an organization serving diverse stakeholders in a globally competitive marketplace.

Blame never solves a problem—it simply shields a person from accepting responsibility. It is the avenue of choice for cowards without the courage to take a chance, the fortitude to take a stand, and the will to make a difference. Problems are solved by innovative and well-reasoned ideas, along with the willingness to pay any price and bear any burden to implement those ideas in a too-often unwilling and ungrateful public. While one book cannot solve all of society's ills, it can help solve one. This book endeavors to take a stand and to make a difference about one of society's ills: the conduct and competency of its managers. Through considerable research and debate, six attributes have been identified to raise the conduct and competency of our managers, the first of which is ensuring that a manager likes what he does.

Like What You Do

I have the ambition to do great things in my life, to make a difference for someone or something along my path. It is certainly not easy: achieving such ambitions takes dedication, drive, sacrifice, and an unbelievable amount of work. Psychologists may offer a theory or two as to source of such ambitions in one's life—whether they derive from some insecurity in one's childhood or in order to gain a sense of self-worth or importance into adulthood—but my unscientific belief is that what drives me is that I truly like what I do.

I am fortunate. Nearly every day I look forward to my day job as a city human resources manager. Why? Where else can you congratulate someone who has just got married or had a child (as it is our office that employees visit to add family members to their benefits). Or help an employee who is struggling to learn certain aspects of his or her job (our office can provide training on how to raise your knowledge and skills). Or, hire a new employee or promote a current employee, thus changing the very nature of his or her life. To be fair, there are surely negative aspects of my job, including denying an employee a raise, dealing with an employee who was injured on the job, or terminating an employee. I choose, though, to only remember the good in my job and to believe that I have a unique opportunity to help those eager to listen and learn new techniques and strategies, those willing to work the hardest and those prepared to sacrifice their time to become the best in their field and who are the most deserving of their rewards. My job provides an outstanding opportunity to work with, and work for, those seeking a better opportunity and a better life.

For the past fifteen years, I have also taught college part-time. To me, the rewards of this position rival if not exceed that of my position in human resources. First of all, excelling as a college instructor requires me to remain current in my field, which typically involves an exorbitant amount of reading. But I love to read. Second, it requires an exorbitant amount of energy to write lesson plans and materials for class. And I love to write. Finally, it requires an extraordinary amount of time conversing with students, debating the intricate theories of the course, and providing valuable feedback to the class on how to become better readers, writers, professionals, and, more importantly, people. All in all, I truly enjoy what I do.

I am a born worker, and I spend my time doing work that I love to do. I am so very fortunate; indeed, I am blessed. What is baffling, however, is why so few can say the same, which is a truly mystifying phenomenon. Granted, there are times in your life where you find yourself in a situation or circumstance not necessarily of your choosing, whether that results from a divorce or illness or business failure. A potential devastating circumstance is almost inevitable at some point. I believe, though, that most such circumstances are temporary. Most recovery from an illness; most find love again; and most find another job. It is during these times, however, that your resiliency is tested, where your true character is determined and revealed. It is also during these times that you are presented with certain choices in life that allow you to begin anew and give you a chance to follow your dreams.

And, so, we return to the question as to why so few like what they do, whether that be in their job, their profession, their industry, even their life? If they don't like what they do, why do they keep doing it? Though, as I mentioned earlier, I'm not a psychologist (or sociologist, or anthropologist, or any other "gist," who has spent years studying human behaviors or emotions), I believe there are three reasons why people choose a job they do not like, a profession they are disinterested in, and an industry that offers them little excitement.

The first reason people choose a job they do not like, a profession they are disinterested in, and an industry that offers them little excitement is because they have no clear life goal or ambition. They are aimless wonderers without a clear direction, devoid of any motivation or inspiration to follow their dreams. They are lifeless souls who will, most likely, know very little happiness in their professional world coupled with near certain disappointment in their later years as they look back over their lack of professional and personal achievements. This is unbelievably sad, mainly because it is so preventable; it is a circumstance largely of their own choosing.

If you have not searched your soul for that which inspires you and then spent your life following that inspiration, it is doubtful you can find happiness or at the very least like what you do. Those who rarely (or, in some cases, never) dreamed the dream of what they could be, of what they should be, of what they must be, tend to take what is offered them. Thirty years later, they look back over an unimagined and unfulfilled life.

At first, I thought this lack of a clear life goal or ambition could be generational. My parents and most of their friends did not display an intense desire or passion to do or be something. That generation was more interested in attaining some semblance of economic security after the Depression and normalcy after World War II. For my mother's generation, careers for women were still somewhat limited, so such thoughts were foreign—the most possible was typically a career as a wife and mother. My father's generation usually followed the paths of their own father or friends. College was still somewhat of a luxury and not necessarily required to obtain a solid, middle-class lifestyle, as most jobs or industries centered around manufacturing, which did not require a college education. Under these circumstances, it is understandable why a life's goal or purpose may not be a priority.

My generation (born in the 1960s and 1970s) was raised in much different circumstances. We did not face catastrophic influences such as the Great Depression and the Vietnam War that fundamentally altered our economic, political, and social worlds. We had relative economic stability and political and social harmony (though the influences of the Vietnam War and civil-rights movement were significant events in our nation's history, they were not the global phenomena of the Great Depression and World War II). That should have provided my generation with a unique opportunity to pursue our ambitions. Instead, some of my friends and acquaintances did not choose the career or profession that interested them and that they were passionate to pursue. They chose professions—for the most part—that offered them little excitement and satisfaction. It is an ironic twist of fate: when a generation was presented with a unique opportunity to pursue its dreams, so many failed to capitalize.

The opportunity passed them by, with nothing to blame for their fate other than their own unwillingness to dream the dream. That brings up the second reason people choose jobs and professions that they do not like: the lack of courage. To put it bluntly, they lacked the guts to stay the course, weather every storm, and overcome any adversity. They lacked the fortitude because they thought the price to pay—in terms of money, relationships, travel, friendships, ego, self-esteem, etc.—was too great to follow their dream. This lack of courage robbed the world of something great. I firmly believe every person is blessed with some talents unique to their person. The failure to perfect that talent—both for the person and our community—is a tragic loss, resulting mainly from an individual's inability to pay the price to follow one's dream and to master his or her fear of failure.

Fear is such a destructive emotion: the fear of failure, the fear of success, the fear of uncertainty, the fear of losing friends and family, the fear of honesty, and the most destructive fear of all, the fear of what others think. These fears create doubt and uncertainty and paralyze one's ambition. For what? So you do not lose? So people like you? I would rather lose everything as I pursue my own dreams and aspirations than win nothing because I settled and pursued someone else's dream or aspiration. In either case, you lose, but far better to lose in the pursuit of something meaningful and worthwhile to you, rather than in the pursuit of fame, fortune, or acceptance from someone else. Be true to your own ambitions, pursue something important to you, and you will never experience failure because there is never any shame in trying, in giving your best, in extending every effort in the pursuit of something that defines who you are.

The grander the dream, the greater the sacrifice required to reach it. There is little wonder, then, that few reach their dreams: the sacrifice is too great. Those who aspire to hold elective office or attend medical school, for example, soon realize the demands on their time, along with the financial resources required to achieve that ambition. These are far from an easy quest, and the sacrifices required cause many to temper their ambitions to more "realistic" aspirations.

It is a shame, for we can never benefit from what could have happened had theses people had the guts to follow through and to pay the price required to achieve grand ambitions.

The final reason people fail to choose a career or profession they like is one that they have less control over: the lack of encouragement. Behind so many successful people are those who aided their journey, whether they were grandparents, parents, teachers, coworkers or friends. Oftentimes, a simple encouraging word or deed may be all that is needed for a person to continue along an often treacherous path to achieve something that is important to them.

Looking back over my own life, I recognize there are some individuals who provided encouragement and guidance to me as I dared to achieve mighty things. I remember the time they took to provide advice and counsel; most importantly, though, I appreciate that they simply cared enough to remind me the journey is worthwhile and that I really can attain my dreams. I remember friends such as Keith Williams, who bought fifty copies of my second book and distributed them to clients in an effort to publicize my efforts—what a gesture. And then are John and Rachel Ellis, who have made me feel a part of their family for fifteen years. There are few times I've enjoyed more than kicking back with John by his pool talking about the goods and bads, the tragedies and triumphs, of life; I'm so fortunate.

There have been people who have cared enough to offer an encouraging word or hand as I strove to achieve my dreams. I hope, too, to pay it back, and even "pay it forward" by offering a hand to those struggling to achieve their own dreams. In my home and office I keep a quotation by William Penn, whose presence and

writings served as an inspiration for the United States Constitution. He wrote:

> I expect to pass through life but once. If, therefore, there be any kindness I can show, or any good thing I can do for any fellow being, let me do it now and not defer or neglect it, as I shall not pass this way again.

Mr. Penn believed the path to glory is not only achieved through your own ambitions, but in helping others achieve theirs as well. Being the sole inhabitant on "Superstar Island" is a lonely existence, no matter the achievements you have catalogued to get there. Hitting the game-winning home run in the ninth inning of the seventh game of the World Series would be a hollow victory if there were no one to clap as you round the bases. Instead of looking solely inward, encourage others to achieve their ambitions as you achieve your own; if you do so, the thrill of your shared experiences will far exceed any solitary and lonely feat you may achieve.

SUMMARY: LIKE WHAT YOU DO

Why people spend their life in a job that brings so little enjoyment is mystifying. As the clock ticks on your time on this earth, it is truly sad to do that which you do not enjoy or that which does not leave you with a sense of pride and accomplishment.

There are some that say they are in a job they dislike because they have little choice. They may have a family to support, or they may not have the qualifications for a more rewarding job, or the job opportunities are not plentiful in their community. They may not have the time to search for another job, or they are too stubborn to reassess their skills and retrain for a different job, or they find it simply too easy and irresistible to blame someone else for their fate. It is a neat trick: lack the time, be stubborn, and blame someone else for the choices you have made in your life. These excuses are temporary at best, because I honestly believe we live in a country where someone can change their circumstances and the trajectory of their life. Eventually the stark reality appears to be that you controlled your own destiny, and you wasted your opportunity.

Just as you often choose the family that you need to support (for example, a spouse or children), you can choose a different lifestyle that may allow you to gain the qualifications necessary for better job. This may require consider financial and social sacrifices to return to college, or to invest your life savings in some type of risky business, or to move to where job opportunities are more plentiful. But, it can be done. Great accomplishments and great rewards usually come from great sacrifice. It is a risk that people must take if they are to achieve something worthwhile and meaningful in their lives.

Good managers, like the good employee, like their jobs, professions, and industries. And, if they do not, they have choices: they can quit or assume ownership and responsibility for their future, take an unbiased assessment of their own skills and abilities in order to upgrade appropriately, and do something to change the direction of their life. We live in a great country, one where you can always improve your position in life through hard work, diligence, and dedication. It simply takes the will and ambition to take advantage of life's possibilities.

Knowledgeable

In the United States, most houses are built on a base of concrete. Concrete is a strong, sturdy, and reliable foundation that supports the weight and various uses of a house for decades. In management, the foundation upon which managers rely upon to perform their duties is knowledge. Knowledge—both in terms of education and experience—provides the strongest, sturdiest, and most reliable foundation for managers to undertake their responsibilities, primarily in their most critical role of making the right decision at the right time and for the right reason.

The higher the position you assume, the greater the importance of knowledge in performing your duties. We expect a police officer to have a working knowledge of the applicable laws, statutes, and ordinances of their jurisdiction. We expect a doctor to have expert knowledge in the field of medicine. And we expect the president of the United States to have an intricate knowledge of government and political processes. We expect this breadth and depth of knowledge in these and other similar managerial positions because the decisions that these individuals make have wide-ranging repercussions for our own and society's future.

Accumulating the knowledge necessary for managers to excel in their positions—including their ability to make the right decision for the organization at the right time and for the right reason—requires an investment of time, effort, and sacrifice, along with the unwavering desire to find the right answer, regardless of preconceived biases, perceptions, and assumptions. Their academic background, along with their professional and personal experiences, plays an integral role in providing the requisite knowledge needed for a position, as does having a clear understanding of the job, the profession, and the industry. Let us start first with the importance of an academic background in making informed and competent decisions.

ACADEMIC BACKGROUND

Education, in general, provides a manager with various knowledges that can be used to make a better decision. Take history as an example. Napoleon had ambitions to control Europe. However, his version of conquering Europe included Russia. Unfortunately, the harsh Russian winter killed a great majority of Napoleon's army, and he lost that war. It was the wrong decision at the wrong time and for the wrong reasons.

Almost 130 years later—during World War II—Germany tried a strategy similar to Napoleon and invaded Russia during the winter months. Adolf Hitler had hoped to reach a strategic victory before the winter months, but he miscalculated. The invasion continued into the winter months, and his army was decimated his army in a similar fashion as Napoleon's. To a large degree, he did not heed the lessons of Napoleon's failure and became destined to repeat it.

Another example that can be learned from education relates to the arts. We learn that pictures, radio, books, video, and the Internet are powerful influences over the human mind. An innovative marketing and promotional campaign can sway the buying patterns of the general public. For instance, an advertisement for a movie that captures the interest of its intended audience can be the difference between a blockbuster and a failure. A book detailing how one should live their life can have a profound impact on the decisions that one makes. Art is a powerful influence in our world; one only needs to review the tens of billions of dollars spent through print, radio, and television by advertisers.

In times previous, a high-school diploma was regarded as the absolute minimum scholastic achievement for those then in the workplace, and it generally signifies that the individual has gained the following competencies:

- Capability to perform elementary mathematical computations.

- Ability to read and interpret the written language, along with the ability to communicate (both orally and in writing) in the appropriate language.

- Awareness of the basic economic, political, and social institutions of your nation and the ability to interact in society accordingly.

- A sense of discipline and self-control, including adhering to the nation's fundamental laws and supporting society through tax contributions.

- The minimum skills and abilities to obtain an entry-level job in the workplace.

While a high-school diploma provided the basic skills and abilities for those in the workplace at that time, the continuing complexity of the workplace (computerization, diverse workplace in terms of employees and customers, telecommunications, etc.) coupled with an increasingly competitive global marketplace requires a greater breadth and depth of educational achievements today than the traditional high-school diploma. Back in the day, a high-school diploma provided sufficient knowledge for one to perform basic functions. No more. Today, many positions require a level of knowledge that is more often attained through college.

Thus, higher education assumes a greater role in today's business world. This education tends to concentrate on three particular areas, which underlie the importance of the managerial position. First, being well-read—it is difficult to be successful in your position if you do not have the requisite information. Books and other literature provide the information that one can use to, among other things, make a better decision. Second, rhetoric, which is defined as speaking eloquently or the ability to articulate your point of view to your audience in an effective manner. Lastly, logic, or the rigid and comprehensive debate and analysis of an issue or problem is a required knowledge.

Today, there lies a schism between those who have a college degree and those who do not. Statistics indicate that those who have a college degree make nearly double, on average, than those who do not have a college degree. Most positions that are financially rewarding tend to require, or expect, a college degree, including doctors, lawyers, architects, engineers, scientists, astronomers, teachers, and accountants.

Highly technical and complex professions require knowledge that is more often than not acquired through intensive studying in a college degree program. We expect accountants to pass a test attesting to their knowledge of tax law, engineers to obtain certification attesting to their knowledge of engineering concepts, and attorneys to pass the bar attesting to their understanding of legal matters. We expect, and demand, these licenses and degrees because they certify that the individual possesses the requisite knowledge to make competent decisions in their field.

The same is expected of a manager. If an individual with a high school diploma is able to perform the functions of his or her job similar to those performed by an individual with a college degree, there would be no reason to pay the money to employ the person with a college degree. It is because the skills and abilities that a person acquires through college that account for much of the income disparity between one who has a college degree and one who does not.

These advanced, comprehensive skills and knowledge will remain at the forefront of the managerial profession for some time, especially as the complexity of the position continues to advance. Today, the complexity of managing a business that interfaces with marketing, finance, accounting, information technology, human resources, public relations—and a host of managerial abilities such as communication, motivation, and conflict resolution—often necessitates that a person possess more advanced knowledge and skills. A college education is not the sole avenue to obtain these knowledge and skills, but it is increasingly difficult to obtain such knowledge in any other manner.

PROFESSIONAL AND PERSONAL EXPERIENCES

In 1988, George Herbert Walker Bush ran for president of the United States. His campaign showcased his experience in the business and governmental worlds over the previous forty years. He was a business owner, a congressman, the chairman of the Republican National Committee, the ambassador to China, the director of the Central Intelligence Agency, and the vice president of the United States. The implication was that such experiences provided the future President Bush with knowledge and that he was the most qualified person for the job.

Conversely, in 2008, Barrack Obama ran for president of the United States on a much different platform. He had virtually no business experience and had held only one national office, that of a United States senator (for two years at the time he announced his candidacy for the presidency). His campaign promised to reform Washington and to change the way business was done, so in some ways experience was seen as a negative attribute, especially in contrast to his more experienced opponent, Senator John McCain. That President Obama's experiences provided him with less knowledge on how government was conducted and the scope and manner in which the inefficiency and incompetency of the system should be addressed was actually seen as a positive trait by most of the voting populace.

In both campaigns, experience was a significant factor in their election, one because of the comprehensive nature of his experience (Bush) and the other because of his lack of experience (Obama), who offered a fresh, untarnished viewpoint of government. One may conclude that experience is not central to the election of a president, but that be more a sign of the times rather than a general statement on the value of experience. Why? Many presidents have had significant leadership experience, whether that be in the political or business worlds; they previously served as vice presidents, governors, generals, and senators. Today, the worlds of business and politics are simply too complex for one to lead and manage without a solid understanding of the rules of what is often called, "the game."

Education is an important avenue to provide the foundation for learning the theories and concepts related to the rules, systems, processes, and cultures of the political and business worlds. An integral part of success is missing, though: the ability to gauge the affect, impact, and success of these theories and concepts in the real world. This is called experience. A perfectly developed plan will remain perfect until it is implemented, and then inevitably adjustments to the plan become a necessity. This is where breadth and depth of one's experience becomes so important: experienced managers are able to better assess and gauge the challenges and obstacles that they may face as an organization implements new, innovative, and sometimes controversial plans and strategies.

The boxer Mike Tyson once said that, "the fight changes with the first punch," and, "everyone has a plan until they get punched in the mouth." Another famous military quote that, "war changes with the first bullet." Both these statements emphasize that you must first study and develop a competent plan in which experience plays a critical role. At this stage, you implement the plan, and immediately you have much less control because it is so incredibly difficult to assess, predict, and interpret in advance the reaction your plan will elicit once executed. Inevitably, it is at this point that the plan's best intentions go awry and where the value of experience plays a central role. Two examples may help illustrate this dilemma, one drawn from the military and the other from business.

First, the military. By nearly all accounts, the 2003 United States invasion of Iraq was a spectacular success. In a matter of weeks, President Saddam Hussein was deposed with the U.S. military largely vanquishing the once feared Iraqi military apparatus. It was a grand military achievement, raising the profiles of Secretary of Defense Donald Rumsfeld and General Tommy Franks to rock-star status.

Though the invasion worked nearly perfectly, the peacekeeping phase of the war has been perceived—by most—as ill conceived and poorly implemented. Why? The general consensus appears to be that the United States overestimated the military capabilities of Iraq and expected a prolonged military campaign and so was not quite ready for the peacekeeping aspect of the war. Finally, the Bush Administration believed it would be seen as liberators and the peacekeeping efforts would be minimal. Without a doubt, miscalculations were made, but it is a showcase example on how difficult it is to assess and determine how someone (or an entire nation) will respond to a given situation, let alone a catastrophic one.

Another example of how unpredictably a plan's outcome may be relates to my experience working as a human resources manager for a municipality. A number of projects and plans have been proposed to increase the efficiencies of government operations or the effectiveness of some service delivery. In one instance, a new software system was purchased, thereby reducing the need for employees to work overtime on a regular basis. In another instance, the municipality reduced low-priority services and consolidated other functions in an effort to reduce staff and, therefore, be able to lower fees and taxes for citizens. In both instances, the municipality met with considerable resistance by employees and their unions, who were concerned about their lack of overtime and promotion opportunities.

Importantly, if the outcome of a plan is difficult to predict, so is human behavior. As a former tennis player, I recall those players who were stellar ball hitters in the practice rounds but became tense and nervous during an actual match. It is an interesting conundrum: their talent was without question, but they were unable to execute once the ball was in play. If you watch two individuals in practice, you may easily determine the stronger player. But, once the game begins, the pressure of competing may affect the best players' ability to use his talent and thus change the outcome of the match. Such is the challenge of predicting not only the outcome of a plan but human behavior as well.

This is why education and experience can play such key roles in the success of a manager. Education provides the foundation, or talent, for a manager. Without education, you have little knowledge to develop your theories and strategies for the workplace. Without experience, you have little knowledge how best to implement and execute those learned theories and strategies, providing an organization with the best opportunity to achieve its ambitions. Experience, then, is built upon that education.

Obtaining the necessary education is fairly simple; the United States has an abundance of educational opportunities to pursue along with a prevalence of government-sponsored educational grants and loans to pay for it. Obtaining the necessary professional experience, however, is not nearly as simple. The best experience has sufficient breadth and depth to provide people with a well-rounded, comprehensive understanding of their job, their company, and their industry. Let us start with knowledge of your job.

KNOWLEDGE OF YOUR JOB

Continual or lifelong learning has become a well-known phrase in the workplace. It means that employees are required to continually upgrade their knowledge and skills to remain competitive. Technology is advancing at a rapid rate, forcing employees to incessantly retain and upgrade their skills. How does one do so? There are a number of avenues one can pursue to remain competitive in their job, including:

Read, read, and read. Read business or other trade magazines that deal with your profession, its future, and the requirements for successful participants in the future.

Network with colleagues. Develop and maintain positive relationships with your coworkers and subordinates. Most employees have a specialty; learn from their specialty and increase your own overall skills and knowledge.

Build a relationship with your supervisor. Those who have advanced in an organization have done so because they have succeeded along their path. Conversing with your supervisors is an outstanding opportunity to learn from their successes, and failures, along with the obstacles they faced.

Learn new and innovative management techniques. Management—being more art than science—is not lacking in books and articles detailing the challenges in the professions, including compensation, motivation, recruiting, and strategic planning. The key is to read a wide range of books and magazines that discuss various management strategies and techniques and then adapt and modify that strategy to meet your particular culture and environment.

KNOWLEDGE OF YOUR COMPANY

The knowledge gained from thoroughly understanding your organization can be significant. Attending meetings, reading corporate literature (such as financial statements and press briefings), and conversing with fellow employees provide insight into the inner workings of the company, which can shed light on your organization and its direction. For instance, had employees at Arthur Anderson Consulting, MCI, and Enron studied and scrutinized their own organization more carefully they may have seen the warning signs of the pending implosions. Doing so might have saved not only an employee's life savings but, in some cases, their careers.

Learning about your organization also highlights the culture of the organization, or "how we do things around here," which is helpful as you enter and progress through an organization. Organizations have developed formal and informal processes and procedures on how to talk, act, interact, and work. These facilitate the interactions between staff and the accomplishment of work objectives. However, this culture can also be debilitating in that it can inhibit change in the process and direction of the organization, change that can allow an organization to adjust to the changing demands of the marketplace.

Especially if you are a new employee, learning about how they do things around you allows you to adjust to a new environment and to become part of another club or fraternity. Then, as you progress through the organization and become more aware of its culture, it is hoped that you may make efforts to mold and transform the organization's culture to reflect the changing competitive environment. Tremendous skill and ability is needed at this stage: the organization has been designed to encourage the current culture and has built natural impediments to any modifications. As an example, in an organization that I am familiar with, new employees quickly learn to follow the direction of more seasoned employees; they soon overlook the mistakes of their fellow employees and avoid challenging a system that has proven financially beneficial to its employees. To not follow the existing culture would risk being ostracized from their organization and, in some cases, affect the perception of their performance and ability to advance in the organization. If you are in a similar situation, at that stage, you may find that this is not the organization you would like to be a part of, or you may search for opportunities to change the culture better reflect your beliefs or those of society.

Learning common goals, language, and procedures is a vital component of understanding an organization's culture and even more so the organization's ability to adapt its culture to the changing marketplace. Certainly learn and respect an organization's culture, but work artfully to ensure the culture is designed or redesigned to enable the organization to best meet the expectations of its customers and stakeholders

KNOWLEDGE OF YOUR INDUSTRY

A glaring deficiency of managers, in my opinion, is their general lack of understanding of their industries. Few managers are aware of the economic, political, and social trends of their industry; similarly, they are unaware of similar trends throughout the United States and international community. This is unfortunate, as it is difficult to make a rational, reasoned decision if you are unaware of the various influences in your industry along with the repercussions of your decisions within the larger business environment.

Today, obtaining a better understanding of your industry is only limited by your time and effort. The information is fairly easy to obtain through a variety of avenues, including the Internet, newspapers, magazines, and books. Managers that familiarize themselves with the specific and general trends of their industry—including the broader economic, political, and social influences—can enable a manager to make decisions more in congruence with these existing trends. Specific trends and influences that a manager should become more knowledgeable and familiar with include:

Globalization.   Today, approximately 30 percent of the world's Gross National Product (GNP) is either an import or an export (triple that of twenty-five years ago). I believe the globalization of business is the preeminent issue of our day. Outsourcing is a direct consequence of globalization: advancements in technology and communication have made it much easier to make and transport goods and services between countries. As a result, a great number of manufacturers have moved their operations to Mexico or overseas to take advantage of the lower labor costs, reduced environmental costs, and minimal regulations.

One of the disadvantages of globalization and outsourcing has been the relentless pressure on employee costs. Middle-class jobs are slowly disappearing as products are being manufactured overseas. This has caused political, economic, and social instability, as the American consumer demands the lowest-priced goods and services, and it is a challenge to produce these goods and services in the United States given our high labor costs.

For the most part, the less advanced knowledge, skills, and abilities required to produce a good or service, the more likely the business will see the lower labor costs that can be found overseas. It makes less sense to manufacture these products and services here in the United States when labor costs can be as much as 90 percent cheaper in other countries.

If United States corporations do not take advantage of the lower wage-labor costs in other countries, they quickly find themselves at a financial disadvantage to foreign competitors, who would produce similar good and services and export them to the United States. United States companies, then, move overseas to produce these products and services to take advantage of the lower costs. So, in reality, manufacturers leaving the United States are doing so more for survival in an increasingly competitive business environment than simply to maximize their profits.

A second consequence of globalization is the inability to determine, account for, and control your competition. When you control industries (cars, airplanes, etc.), you can better dictate the factors of competition. These factors would include price, customer services, and level of quality. In 1950, the United States made approximately 75 percent of the world's vehicles. We dominated the auto industry as well as many others mainly because our competitors were decimated by World War II. General Motors could build nearly any car (for any price and quality) and still expect to sell that vehicle. They could provide generous benefits and job security to their employees (thereby expanding the middle class) and it would not put their business at a competitive disadvantage in relation to its competitors because everyone in that industry offered similar benefits and job security.

That is no longer the case. General Motors wage costs are much greater than Toyota's (or other foreign firms) because of General Motors generous health and retirement benefits. Toyota does not offer this level of benefits for its United States based workers, and thus its costs are lower. General Motors cannot dictate that every participant in the industry offer similar benefits (as in the 1950s); thus, it cannot control the factors of competition and is at a disadvantage in relation to its competitors, unless it brings its costs in line with its competitors. This is a primary reason we see wages, health insurance, and retirement benefits falling for the average American worker. It is also a reason why General Motors eventually filed for bankruptcy protection and was rescued by the federal government.

Increasing competitive business environment. A competitive advantage is a situation in which a business does something better than its competitor. It is the main reason that a customer purchases a product or service from one business rather than the other. For instance, a customer may stay at a Ritz Carlton rather than a Hyatt because of the image of wealth and exclusivity of a Ritz Carlton. That would be the competitive advantage of the Ritz.

In previous times, the Ritz Carlton could maximize the return on its competitive advantage for a number of years without the worry that its competitors would catch up. Once one business gains a competitive advantage, other businesses take note and make quick adjustments to their own business strategies to become more competitive.

Today, the innovative product of tomorrow is often matched or exceeded within a brief time (often a matter of weeks). Though the expense expended to gain this competitive advantage can often be considerable, the timeframe to exploit that advantage in the marketplace is often brief. Once a company garners a competitive advantage, its competitors can more easily determine the source of that competitive advantage, mainly because information is more available and easily disseminated throughout the world. This provides competitors with a wealth of information on others within their specific industry. The result is that you may not gain your investment back in a timely fashion. Additionally, it reinforces the mandate that you must constantly innovate your product or service. The age of resting on your laurels is truly over.

Quality product and service. The term, "quality," refers to expectations. Quality products and service, then, mean that your product and service meet the expectations of your customers.

There are few trends more important today than to produce a quality product or to offer a quality service. Given the numerous competitors in nearly every industry, an important variable that differentiates you from your competitor is quality. Managers must constantly study their competitors and survey their customers to ensure that the highest quality is obtained and never compromised. Consumers will usually pay more for quality; low quality is usually the quickest way to bankruptcy for a business and the unemployment line for its employees.

SUMMARY: KNOWLEDGE

"Knowledge is power"—this is a famous phrase, often interpreted as the more knowledge you acquire the greater importance and worth you attain in a given situation. Competing organizations typically have the same access to technology and financial resources. However, they do not have equal access to people. Those organizations that are the most innovative and remain at the forefront of their industry are those with employees who have the greatest knowledge. This allows them to think differently, to explore and invent, and to constantly reinvent and invigorate their product and service. It can be the key difference between one organization and another.

Those managers with the greatest breadth and depth of knowledge have a better chance to make the right decision at the right time and for the right reason. Without that knowledge, you have to rely on attitudes, emotions, assumptions, and perceptions. How often have we relied on our attitudes, emotions, assumptions, and perceptions to make a decision only to find that if we had the right knowledge—through a combination of education and experience—we would have made a much different, much better decision?

Seeking a broader and more substantive education is a vital first step to providing yourself with the background to assess and determine a course of action. Then, you must acquire a similarly broad, diverse experience so that you can execute your plan. It is similar to Roger Federer, the great tennis player, who studied the great serves, volleys, forehands, and backhands (collectively known as the tennis basics) of former champions to assess how to hold a racquet, toss a tennis ball before serving, and bend his knees before striking a forehand. Then, he had to put what he learned into practice, which meant he had to gain extensive experience in hitting a serve, a volley, a forehand, and a backhand. This combination produced a champion tennis player. In business, it produces champion decision making, which is a vital attribute of a good manager.

Solid Organizational Skills

Once the dreams and aspirations of an organization's leadership team are determined, the organization's future lies in the hands of its managers. It is primarily through the organization's managers that these aspirations are achieved. Managers are charged with translating the often lofty ambitions of its leaders into a workable action plan. This requires a certain managerial skill set, one that becomes the foundation of the managerial profession. Similar to the role a cement foundation plays for a home, unless a manager have a strong set of skills to serve as their foundation the organization is challenged to survive over the long term without managers skilled in these areas.

The skill set that should be at the core of every manager's position coalesces into what I call organizational skills. I believe there are three: ability to plan, ability to delegate, and ability to manage time.

ABILITY TO PLAN

If you do not know where you are going, you will likely end up somewhere, it just may not be where you want to go! Planning provides focus and direction, and for managers it is a crucial skill that ensures that an organization's resources are not misplaced or misallocated and are instead directed towards the right end.

In general, planning is defined as the design of the hoped-for future. Once the organization's objective and direction are determined by the leadership team, managers are delegated the responsibility to plan the organizational structures and practices that galvanize a workforce to attain that objective in an efficient and effective manner. In other words, it starts with the organization's leadership team determining the objectives of the organization, then followed by the managers determining how to get there. This plan, created by managers, is intended to provide a common and worthwhile direction to the employees, ensure that every action has a consequence that moves the organization closer to this stated objective, and that any obstacles or impediments are identified early and mitigated promptly.

Experienced planners follow five steps, or guidelines, to ensure the planning process is smooth, fluid, and effective. First, they clearly understand the objective. Too often the manager has accomplished an objective—even in an efficient and effective manner—but it was the wrong objective. If they do so, the misallocation of precious resources in today's highly competitively global environment can cause a severe strain throughout the organization. So, be very clear about where the organization is headed and the objective to be achieved, so that everyone is rowing in the same direction.

Second, planners understand organizational basics, including how to structure an organization, how to manage organizational behavior, and how to develop and promote a favorable organizational culture. In essence, it is the planner who creates an organization with the intended consequence of taking advantage of the abilities of the organization and its people. A manager does not need to be an expert in all aspects of an organization, but it is nearly impossible to develop and implement a competent plan without some knowledge and experience of an organization.

Third, planners need the foresight to identify impediments and obstacles to their success. The ability to identify a challenge before it appears and wreaks havoc within the organization is critical to an organization's stability and viability. The ability to think broadly and comprehensively when developing a plan cannot be overstated.

Fourth, competent planners have the ability to adapt. Most like to think of themselves as adaptable or flexible, but in my opinion those traits are more the exception rather than the rule because they require managers who can control their egos and admit that they may have made a mistake and managers who have the courage, strength, and self-confidence to adjust a plan that they may have originally staked their reputation on.

Adaptation is an interesting challenge, which is one reason plans fail; in the face of evidence that the plan is not producing the desired results, few have the ability to change course and embark on a previously unforeseen direction. It takes courage and the willingness to admit to a mistake and the confidence in a new course to ensure that the organization's plan adapts to the changing reality of the situation. This is a rare find in a planner.

Fifth, experienced planners are positive and enthusiastic. We live in an increasingly complex and destabilizing world, one in which a brighter tomorrow is less assured than in previous times and in which the ability to better our standard of living—just as our predecessors did—seems to be more of a myth rather than a reality. I believe it is more difficult now to raise your standard of living, and it is becoming increasingly difficult for people to advance their status in life without an unbelievable focus, ambition, and the strength of character that they may have developed through the years. Planners are aware of these difficulties, the negative thoughts and actions of employees, and the challenging and changing global marketplace. The best planners are those who continually state, "yes we can" and "we'll make it," as opposed to thoughts similar to, "can it really work?" or, "it's the best we can do at this time." Importantly, a plan without the hope to achieve it is really no plan at all.

I attended a speech by Ann Richards, the former governor of Texas, several years when she said, "Fools rush in where fools have been before." I have never forgotten that wise statement, and it goes to the heart of planning: devote the time and energy to plan your future and develop the patience and fortitude to stay on that path, or adapt as necessary, through the inevitable obstacles. Let some other manager or organization be the fool and rush into a future that is ill-conceived and ill-planned.

ABILITY TO DELEGATE

Organizations consist of individuals working collaboratively to accomplish a task or goal. As mentioned previously, while organizational leaders are charged with determining the direction of the organization, it is the managers who determine how to get there. They do so by allocating the tasks and assignments among the resources of the organization in the hope that the accomplishment of these tasks will enable the organization to reach its goals. In essence, managers spend much of their time allocating—or delegating—tasks among their employees, first by identifying the most appropriate person to delegate to, then by motivating that individual to accomplish this task, and finally by ensuring that task was accomplished efficiently and effectively.

Some managers hesitate to delegate for a number of reasons, mainly because the manager:

- believes it is easier to do the task themselves

- may be a perfectionist

- may want the credit for the work

- may not want to impose on others

- may have little confidence in the person they are delegating to.

Other managers may have little hesitation in delegating work to others, recognizing that their time is better spent performing their managerial functions rather than the functions that should be delegated to their subordinates. Their strategy, however, should revolve around more than finding a warm body to assign the work to, and instead ensure that someone properly trained and competent performs that task.

Delegating work is important because it is one of the few mechanisms by which management can develop subordinates. It allows managers to evaluate and broaden the knowledge and skills of their employees, subordinates to accept greater responsibilities, and the decentralization of the workplace to make an organization more nimble and flexible. It also allows the manager to do more productive work. Generally speaking, managers are not paid to *do* the work, but rather to ensure the work is done through a wide variety of resources (whether those resources are employees, consultants, computers, contractors, technology, etc.). Managers that perform lower-level tasks often do so because they lack the knowledge and skills to properly delegate, which can have serious consequences for an organization. This may inadvertently raise salary costs (by overpaying managers to do lower-level tasks), impede the growth of their employees, and cause others in the organization to question the value of that manager.

As with planning, a manager can become a more effective delegator by following a series of strategies and techniques. First, a manager must clearly understand the task to be delegated. It is quite difficult to delegate properly—in effect, to assign the proper task to the proper person—unless you know the task and the type of person needed to accomplish it.

The second delegating strategy is to have a solid understanding of the knowledge, skills, abilities, education, experience, training, and talents of your employees. If you do, you can identify the perfect marriage between the task to be accomplished and the most appropriate person to complete that task.

Third, effective delegators thoroughly explain the task to be accomplished to the employee, including the schedule to complete the task and any additional resources that may be available. Considerable time should be devoted to ensuring that the employee has the necessary training, that there are no outstanding questions or concerns about the task, and that there has been a substantive discussion of any challenges or obstacles that may arise.

Finally, while managers may establish routine checkups and checkpoints, they should get out of the way and allow the employee to utilize his talents to accomplish the task. After all, this is the reason that you selected the person to accomplish the task: you thought they were the most qualified. Let them use their imagination and ingenuity to meet the objectives of the task. If you do so, the employee may surprise you with his creativity.

One other point about delegating: be sure to give credit to the person who actually accomplished the task. To do otherwise can be a catastrophic mistake for a manager, as it destroys the motivation, will, and spirit of your employees. Managers get enough credit when their department accomplishes its objectives; give employees the credit when they accomplish their own good deeds. It is not only fair and just but showcases the inherent goodness of the manager (a subject we talk about in greater detail in the final chapter).

ABILITY TO MANAGE TIME

Because of the often tremendous demands on managers—including the need to interact with their supervisor and colleagues, direct and evaluate the work of their subordinates, and perform their own tasks and responsibilities—an organizational trait of a good manager is the ability to manage time. Nearly anything you want to accomplish in life, either personal or professional, is accomplished through the mechanism of time management. Time has much to do with promise, in that your promise is limited to the amount of time that you have. Huey Long, the Louisiana senator assassinated in 1935, said as he was dying that, "God, don't let me die. I have so much to do." So much promise, yet so little time.

It takes time to apply and interview for a promotion, to maintain a great friendship, or to realize financial security. The burdens of management, including the constant development and revision of complex and often contradictory goals and strategies, require managers to expertly manage their time. So much of what you want to do as a manager and as a person is predicated on the effective use of that time;

manage your time well and you have a greater chance to achieve your life's ambitions.

Effective time management starts with knowing what you want out of life and your goals, that which you were born to accomplish. I sometimes wonder if people spend enough time on their goals. We see fellow employees or friends that may work hard on their jobs, and even prepare for the next promotion, but do they necessarily spend time trying to determine where they want to go? I doubt it. People just tend to do and to go without much thought as to where.

There is an important concept: you need to invest the time to determine what you want to do with the rest of your life. Without goals, you really have no reason to organize yourself and your time because you are not going anywhere in particular. It then makes no difference how long anything takes. You only manage your time because there is something that you want to do with your time. Goals and time are your keys to success: you achieve success—as defined in your goals—through the medium of time. Every goal requires some amount of time, however small, to be achieved. Because the amount of time in your life is limited, you cannot achieve an infinite number of goals.

I believe you should spend ten to fifteen minutes every day assessing and reassessing your life, trying to determine if you are on the right track and consider any movements or changes that you need to make to get you where you want to go. Unless you truly know where you are going, you will spend time moving in a direction that will ultimately not make you happy. That is not a wise course of action and is certainly the start and continuation of a gloomy life. And remember: even if you do not reach your goal, if you are on the road that makes you happy you will always enjoy what you do.

Once you know where you want to go, there are some strategies that are beneficial to better manage your time to then pursue your goals. Here are five of the more prominent strategies that you may want to consider:

First, do things once. When you open an e-mail, either answer it or file it away. Avoid having to open the same e-mail later, which requires you to reread and rethink it. If you open a bill, write the check and address the return envelope (or, better yet, learn to pay your bill through an online payment system, which also saves paper); even if you cannot mail the letter as yet, avoid having to open the bill later to remind yourself of its contents.

Second, use the phone as much as possible to avoid the often time-consuming process of writing. It is quicker to talk than write, and it can be more efficient, since any misunderstandings or misinterpretations are evident when conversing with someone because you have a better opportunity to assess someone's facial expressions or tone of voice. This type of feedback can provide highly advantageous. Furthermore, conversations also provide a person with the opportunity to make personal connection with your listener, whether they be subordinates, customers, suppliers, etc.

Third, list and prioritize your tasks. As mentioned before, make a written schedule or task list. I have never met an organized person who does not have a list of tasks or goals. Great ambitions are complex and multifaceted. There are many different interlocking decisions and actions to make in achieving your ambitions, and unless you possess a photographic memory a written list of prioritized tasks is essential.

A written list provides focus and reduces the stresses in your life. It serves as a constant reminder of the duties and tasks that you need to do; when your mind or ambitions wander, the list reminds you of your direction and of where you intend to direct your life. Moreover, some managers have an unneeded level of stress and anxiety because they fear missing a deadline and dropping the ball on a critical task. The written list creates a level of simplicity in an otherwise harried lifestyle by ensuring all tasks are accounted for, thereby negating the need to rely on memory for upcoming tasks and responsibilities.

In prioritizing tasks, the person who has an innate ability to miss deadlines will have a short life span as a manager; hence, the word "dead" in "deadline." For most managers, they have too much to do and too little time to do it in. Some managers work an exorbitant number of hours, which can take its toll on their physical and emotional well-being. Other managers let some tasks and responsibilities slip; these become casualties of their own ineptitude.

The best managers have learned the art of prioritizing work, whereby they accomplish the most critical first and delegate the lesser important tasks to the appropriate employee (as discussed previously). Prioritization is an art rather than a science, because there are no easy rules one can follow that will transform a person who has an inability to meet deadlines to one that is a well-oiled prioritization machine. It is like losing weight or saving money: it takes dedication and discipline. Though not easy, one can learn to better prioritize their workload (and personal life too) by answering two key questions:

- What date is the task due? Obviously, those tasks with a more imminent due date have a higher priority. Knowing the due date also affords a person the opportunity to better plan when the task can be completed. For example, if a task is due in four days and you estimate the task will take twenty hours to complete, you can devote five hours each of the next four days to complete the task, or ten hours each of the next two days.

■ What is the importance of the task? There are times when we do not know the due date of a task and must use our judgment. In this case, the task to accomplish first is that which has the greatest impact on your organization or stakeholders.

Prioritization is less about learning the art of prioritizing than having the discipline to identify your tasks and ensure that you remain resolute in meeting the obligations of your position. Do the most important priorities, those with the most pressing due date, as soon as practical so that if there are any future unanticipated demands on your time, you have already completed the most important tasks. At a minimum, this is expected of those in the managerial profession.

Four, learn to say no. In time management, it is important that you have a sense of self-discipline. This requires that you have an ability to say no. When you take on more than you can handle, your quality will suffer, so you are better off taking on only what you can comfortably handle. So, when possible, be polite but firm and say no. It may be preferable to give the appropriate reason and offer alternatives to meet the person's need, but if you assume too many responsibilities, it would be a challenge for any person to devote the necessary time to do them properly.

Finally, remember the importance of using small amounts of time. When people look to determine where their money is spent, they often find that a majority of their money is spent in small increments (coffee, lunch, magazines, car washes, junk food, video games, etc.). The same goes for time; a majority of time is wasted in small amounts. Therefore, recapture your time by identifying and utilizing the small amounts of time, whether that is before, during, or after work. During those periods of the day in which you may have a minute or two, organize your desk, answer your e-mails, and pay your bills. You can also double up on tasks (example: listen to a report while driving) and make use of non-peak hours (go to lunch at eleven thirty AM rather than the busy twelve PM time), and use public transportation (which allows you to read and/or write during these periods of time).

SUMMARY: ORGANIZATIONAL SKILLS

No matter the detailed and insightful plan an organization or manager develops, it needs to be implemented. This requires superior organizational abilities and skills that can more easily be learned than some of the other traits of an effective or good manager.

The ability to plan, delegate, manage your time, and prioritize are the basic building blocks upon which a manager relies upon to accomplish his or her tasks. This is where managers develop their reputation for competence and excellence. While the preceding chapters provided strategies to like what you do and to become more knowledgeable about your business, becoming an organized manager will be directly related to your ability to be seen as a "can do, will do" employee and a competent and important component of the organization's continued success.

There exists no perfect strategy that does not first require the will and dedication to think before acting (planning), to be a builder of an employee's talents (delegating), to know your goals and manage your resources to get there (time management), and to meet the most important obligations in a timely manner (prioritizing). Meet these standards and you will have a strong foundation to build upon as a manager.

Work Hard

At some point in life, you have probably admired the performances or achievements of the superstars in their field. I remember listening to President Reagan's stunning, final speech to the nation as president in 1988 and the Reverend Jesse Jackson's stirring "keep hope alive" speech at the 1984 Democratic National Convention. I listen in wonder at the vocal achievements of Christian singer Michael W. Smith. And I remain in awe not only of the shot-making brilliance of the greatest tennis player ever, Roger Federer, but also of the grace in which he lives his life.

Without question, these people are talented. Oratorical eloquence, a musical ear, and deft hand-eye coordination may indeed originate as God given gifts. Rarely, however, are gifts given that are in such abundance and so completely that no training or practice is required to perfect that gift. President Reagan was a former actor—and Reverend Jackson a former preacher—both well rehearsed in public speaking. Michael W. Smith spent years in a recording studio perfecting his sound. And Roger Federer hits hundreds of balls a day in preparation for the Grand Slam tournaments. Talent, yes, but also hard work.

Talent is as important to work as education is to experience. Talent forms the foundation upon which a person can work hard to perfect it. Managers rely on some measure of talent. There are those who are talented speakers and others are natural organizers or have an innate ability to learn complex educational theories and processes. Some talent in your chosen profession or career is a necessity.

Most organizations have the same access to capital, equipment, etc. What they do not have is the same access to is talent: to those people I call superstars. Why superstars? I firmly believe that it is not the stars of an organization that propel it to prominence and that give it its competitive advantage. It is those very few people who have a knowledge, a skill, or an ability that is unique to their industry, or even their world, who possess a sense of greatness that is distinct and exceptional—traits that define who they are and the promise they offer for the future.

These superstars became the dominant force in their fields. These people create the innovative approaches in not only solving the problems of the day, but in dreaming up the catalytic events that will shape the future. Think of any successful company, and you will most likely encounter a few individuals who have shaped the destiny of that firm. They are the builders and dreamers, the ones who transformed what is to what it could be and what it will be.

Those superstars with superb talent are who the organization must search for and ensure never leave the organization. For while many like to say it's the people who are the source of success, in reality it is those few superstars that control the future. Find them and your fate is secure.

Talent, then, is not enough. Good managers possess an attribute similar to Ronald Reagan, Reverend Jackson, Michael W. Smith, and Roger Federer: they also work hard. They are driven to achieve their ambitions, are willing to bear any sacrifice, and are determined to overcome any challenge. It is this combination of drive and determination, along with sacrifice, that separates the common, average manager from the uncommon, good manager.

DRIVE

A driven and determined person is someone who is consumed by what they do. They are often the earliest at work and the last to leave, are willing to assume any responsibility, and display a can-do, will-do attitude in all they do. They are driven to achieve the ambitions that they have set. My children are driven to visit every amusement park in the United States. We have seen nearly all of them, but they remain in the eternal quest to find and ride the tallest and fastest rollercoaster ever built. I hope they will be as driven to go to a great college as a stepping stone to a life full of adventure and accomplishment!

Drive is an attribute common to all; what actually drives each person is not. Some are driven by food, others by money, and others by vengeance and hate. I believe most are driven by some combination of good and evil, love and hate, positivity and negativity, obstruction and contribution, admiration and envy, and confidence and insecurity. Certainly, organizations seek employees driven by positivity, with an ability to make a significant contribution toward the organization's objectives. With managers, the standards and expectations are much higher: organizations that not only seek someone driven by positivity and the ability to contribute but also with the knowledge and skills as presented in this book. These attributes, along with the energy to achieve and sustain them, are hallmarks of good managers.

At times, one's drive may rise unexpectedly. My college roommate and fellow fraternity brother (go Sigma Chi!), Keith Williams, once owned a successful mortgage brokerage company, but his true passion was bike riding. He was always looking to the next race and often traveled across the world to do take part (of course, his beautiful wife, Sarah, and his three boys—Davis, Brendon, and Aiden—came first!). It was fun, but few things in life seem to last. He woke up one day and had pain down his arms and into his chest. Minutes later, he was in the emergency room with heart failure, only to be saved by a pacemaker. This happened to a person with Lance Armstrong-type physical condition, with never a history of heart trouble. He was unbelievably fortunate to have survived.

As so often happens when someone goes through a catastrophic illness or event, Keith reflected on his past, reassessed his present, and pondered his dreams for the future. His life revolved around bicycle racing; he was driven not only to compete as a racer but to share these stories and experiences with the other racers. So what did he do? He summoned the courage and fortitude to sell his mortgage business and—with most of the money he earned from his business—took a chance and opened up an online, bicycle wheel business, titled Williams Cycling (here's a plug for Keith: you can shop at his store at the following website, www.williamscycling.com). Though only in his third year, it has been an unqualified success. He's a driven man doing something he loves (and is even more fortunate to have the unbelievable support of his wife, Sarah).

Another incredibly driven man is my old friend, Bill Munroe. I met Bill over twenty-five years ago in the fraternity (I met some great people there!). I was lucky in that I didn't need to work during college; my parents only demanded that I get good grades. Bill, on the other hand, worked a number of jobs because he had to put himself through college, not only paying his college tuition but his personal living expenses as well. He was always working, trying to make a living at such a young age. Many of us, on the other hand, did not have to work and instead could spend more time with our fellow fraternity brothers enjoying the college experiences, whether that was spending Spring Break at Daytona Beach, Florida, or the Christmas Break on a cruise to Mexico.

In retrospect, it wasn't fair, but I never heard Bill complain and that says a lot about him. He was driven to make a success of his life so that he could give his children (he has two: Jake and Kyra, along with a phenomenally nice wife, Patti) everything he never had. It's was purely unselfish ambition, a reason there are few people I admire more than Bill. He wanted a better life for those who came after him.

After graduating college (with honors no less), Bill embarked on a career in finance. He then transitioned into sales, holding a series of increasingly prominent positions. It was hard work, requiring exorbitant hours that precluded much time with his family and friends. It was a sacrifice he was willing to make in the short run because he believed his family would be rewarded in the long term. And he was right. He built up, and sold, two companies over these years, allowing him to semi-retire before he was forty!

Some say he was lucky; I absolutely disagree. He was singularly focused to succeed and was willing to pay the price to have the opportunity to succeed. Today, he owns the Munroe Consulting Group (another plug for a friend!). He leads an enviable life but only because he was driven to make his ambitions come true. He is a driven man—driven to succeed—and it's great to see a good guy realize his dream.

Some wonder at my own drive. For the past twenty years, I have had three professional ambitions: to work in human resources, teach college, and write books. They have consumed my life, but I would have it no other way. Keith, Bill, and I are fortunate: we are driven to achieve but in professions that we have chosen. Lucky, indeed, but the drive to achieve one's ambition has not come without sacrifice.

SACRIFICE

"You cannot have it all!" "Something has got to give." Infamous words for those with grand ambitions. As we can see, success comes at a price, and that price may be time away from family, lack of genuine friendships because of the dedication to your job, few grand adventures across the globe because of the need to save and invest your money, or declining health because of the escalating stress and lack of time to follow a strict health regimen. Working hard—even at something you like—requires a sacrifice many are only too willing to make in the beginning, but their enthusiasm for their dream diminishes as the sacrifices required to achieve it escalate.

Success demands a greater sacrifice, whether that be starting a business, creating a reputation, or investing the time and effort to climb the corporate ladder. It requires an all-encompassing focus, with success nearly impossible without long work hours. Those who aspire for continued success become well aware of the sacrifices that need to be made: time away from home, the stress and anxiety from a highly-responsible position, and often the envy and jealously of colleagues and subordinates. It is an incredible price to pay and a tremendous sacrifice to bear. Few people I know are willing to pay that price. My friend John Solheim is one such person.

For many years, John served as a vice president of a large business in Northern California. It was a great job, in which he encountered spectacular success and established a legacy at that company that stands the test of time. In 2006, he was offered an outstanding job opportunity at a Fortune 50 organization. The decision to move to another state— away from their home, church, friends, and schools—was difficult, but his family knew the sacrifice would be worthwhile because of the opportunities this new position would offer.

John accepted the job. We miss spending time with him, but he's embarked on a great career with a phenomenal company. Tough people make tough decisions; good people make the right decision. John makes the tough decisions that are also the right ones; for this reason, he leads an increasingly rewarding life for him and his family.

Sacrifices can be a lonely circumstance, but shared sacrifices in the pursuit of something decent and honorable can make for an exhilarating, exciting experience, one that may define your life. Those who avoid the sacrifices that are required in the pursuit of their ambitions end their lives as a dreamer of dreams, rather than a doer of deeds. That is a terrible tragedy.

SUMMARY: WORK HARD

There is no shortage of educated, experienced, and talented people in this world. More Americans have a bachelor's degree than at any time in our nation's history; employees have broader work experience because they transition between jobs and organizations more frequently; and some degree of talent is common to each and every one of us. There is, however, a shortage of educated, experienced, and talented people who have the drive and determination to do something with what they have been given.

Over the years, I have devoted much of my time and effort in the pursuit of my ambitions, and the rewards have been extremely worthwhile. The sense of accomplishment and pride in building a life of meaning far surpasses the sacrifices along the way. And when those sacrifices become great, you hope that there are friends and family who help you shoulder the burden.

Some time ago, work was incredibly consuming, to the point where I questioned—even for a brief moment—whether I would finish this book. I mentioned this to my buddy Sierra Brucia, and a couple days later he sent me the following quote:

> See a man diligent in his business.
> He will stand before kings.

The quote is from Proverbs, and it reinvigorated my ambitions. In fact, this book is a direct result of receiving that quote. It reminded me that I am a worker, always have been and always will be. Hard work and sacrifice may not be the sole predictors of success, but it is increasingly difficult to achieve meaningful success without both. And, at the end of the day, there are few descriptions of a person more welcome than they worked hard at work worth doing. It has consumed my life: to do good work worth doing.

Make Work Fun

My motto, or philosophy of life, is to "always look for the good along the road of life." No matter where we go, or what we do, I constantly remember and recite that phrase. Whether we hear others talk disparagingly about another person, or someone criticizes us, or before we bemoan our own challenges in life, I have repeated that phrase so many times that my kids start to roll their eyes and say, "I know, I know, Dad... always look for the good along the road of life." I'm glad they have learned an important lesson: you should be more grateful about what you do have than ungrateful for what you do not have.

I believe that there is far too much negativity in our world. From television to the business world to our own interactions with our fellow man, there is a greater emphasis on what is wrong than on what you can do to make it right. We concentrate more on who to blame for our fate rather than to commend those who lend a helping hand along the road. We remember, and are affected more by, the bad that happens to us rather than the good—so unfortunate.

I wish more would enjoy the road they travel along their life. There is so much to see and appreciate as you pass the time on this earth. From the majestic snow-capped mountains, to the tranquility of riding horses through the pastures, to the stunning sounds of water flowing through the rivers and streams, images of beauty and wonder fill our landscapes if only we choose to search for the good rather than the evil.

Have a conversation with your family and friends and—most times—you will recount the fun they have had, from visiting friends in the Texas prairies to golfing or the movies. When the conversation turns to work, on rare occasions is the word "fun" actually used. I doubt the words, "I had a blast at work today," or "I cannot wait to get to work tomorrow," or even, "I cannot believe they pay me to do what I do at work; I would do it for free," have been uttered by many or even a few.

For some, saying you had fun at work implies that you did not work or are not serious in your work. In reality, I believe the opposite may be the more truthful. Those who have fun where they work, who they work with, and who they work for, tend to be more motivated and invested in their work. Would it not be great to feel the same about the work as you do about play? That can be done. In today's competitive work environment, it must be done.

I enjoy tennis and golf and strive to get better and better, because the better I get the more I enjoy playing tennis and golf. I wish I had more time to spend playing at these activities; there are few adventures more exhilarating than spending time hitting a tennis ball or crushing a golf ball on the first tee. Life can be fun, if you live it right; some just need a little help to get it right. This is what the good managers are good at doing: helping to make the workplace not only a fun place to accomplish your work but also to be a great place to spend your time. They do so by following three, simple principles:

- First, care about people

- Second, find the right person for the right job

- Finally, have an extraordinary attitude.

CARE ABOUT PEOPLE

Care is the genuine concern about someone else, about their present state and future dreams. It is more than wishing someone good health and good cheer; it is helping them achieve those things as well. There are few people you meet along the path of your life who sincerely care about you and who truly wish you well. In a world where it seems so many are out for themselves—who make choices or decisions that only benefit themselves and their interests—it is unique to find a manager who cares about their employees and who believes an organization can help enable the desires and dreams of its employees.

In the workplace, this might be called mentoring or teambuilding, in which supervisors spend time and effort to develop and encourage employees in their chosen profession. If managers are successful, the workforce is more motivated to achieve its objectives, resulting in greater productivity and profitability for the enterprise and a greater realization of each individual's dreams, goals, and desires. It is a solid argument but lacks one important piece of the puzzle: for employees to be influenced and motivated by a kind and caring manager, employees must feel the manager's interest is unselfish and genuine.

I have worked for two such managers, John Dangberg and Jackie Whitelam. Coincidentally, they both worked at the same firm. John was the executive director of the Capitol Area Development Authority, a state of California and city of Sacramento agency charged with redeveloping the downtown Sacramento area. Jackie was the deputy director. They both were unbelievably considerate. John was the last to criticize and the first to compliment. He hand wrote notes of appreciation for the efforts of his staff, whether they were successful or not. I received one such note from John that I have kept framed on my desk to this day. It reads:

> Thanks Dean, nice work! The follow-up plan is a great way to ensure the healing/learning process is effective and complete. It is great to have someone as competent and thorough heading up our HR.

John is a manager who makes you want to work harder for him and, by extension, work harder for the organization. He is a good man.

Jackie, likewise, is one of the most kind and caring persons I have known. She remembered birthdays and anniversaries, was the first to say hello and goodbye at the office, and asked continually about your friends and family. She would buy a cup of coffee for someone who is having a challenging day or give another employee a plate of cookies or muffins for a job well done. Of course, there was the personal, handwritten note expressing her appreciation and gratitude for not only your work but your contributions to making the workplace a better place. She, more than anyone else at the organization, created the family culture that some claim propelled our organization to achieve such great success.

John and Jackie fostered an environment in which people felt that their contributions were valued and that treating people with the genuine kindnesses of life (saying "hello," or asking a coworker if they could "pick up lunch for you on the way back to work," or wishing everyone "a great weekend") was central to the organization's success. They simply cared about the people they worked with, and in return, most employees enjoyed who they worked for and where they worked. It was a happy place to be and to work, all because of the simple kindnesses of a few people.

John and Jackie realized that when you help others, you help yourself. Employees crave to work for someone who, no matter the time or the occasion, is willing to help them achieve their goals and attain their success. It is a perfect example, most would say, of a good person doing good things for others. We like and admire that conduct because, at some point, we realize we will be the beneficiaries. In other words, we admire the good thoughts and deeds we see people do, because we realize that the goodness they exhibit to other people will one day be extended to us.

And I continue to learn from good managers who cross my path. Blair King, the city manager of the City of Lodi, and David Main, the city's police chief, are two such people. Blair follows four simple rules: don't mess with the money; think; treat people respectfully; and work hard. Yes, work hard. I've included that rule in this book, and he deserves credit for it. David, likewise, stands as a vivid reminder on how to treat employees: always fair; always constructive; always positive; and always encouraging. Few managers meet the standards set by Blair and David, but more could if they follow their examples.

Inevitably, we endeavor to be around people who care because they make us feel important and valued contributors to the organization. They salute our accomplishments, instilling a sense of pride in ourselves and a belief that we can truly make a difference. And when someone cares about you, you tend to care about them in return. Inevitably, employees yearn for such a work environment because it makes them feel good about what they do and who they are. It makes work a rewarding experience and life a fun adventure.

FIND THE RIGHT PERSON FOR THE RIGHT JOB

It is hoped that managers like their work, have some talent to do it, and possess the drive and determination to accomplish their objectives. All are important, but since managers accomplish their objectives primarily through others—their employees—finding and retaining the right employee for the right job is a determining factor in any success they may have. It is also a determining factor in creating and sustaining a fun place to work. Let me explain why.

It is no coincidence that the legendary sports teams, those who won multiple team championships, also had legendary team members. Think of the New York Yankees and the Boston Celtics. These two teams hold the record for the most team championships in baseball and basketball, respectively. The players on those championship teams are among the most hallowed in their sport, earning places in their respective Halls of Fame: Babe Ruth, Lou Gehrig, Mickey Mantle, and Joe DiMaggio for the New York Yankees; Bill Russell, Bill Walton, and Larry Bird of the Boston Celtics. These teams found the right person, for the right position, at the right time.

During their glory years, when the wins far outnumbered the losses, it was not hard to imagine the Yankee and Celtic players having an unbelievable sense of fun. Winning is an incomparable feeling that is created when supremely talented individuals work collaboratively and cooperatively together. The good managers find these gifted individuals and then create a work environment that elicits the talents of each individual for the benefit of the collective.

Whether on the baseball field, the basketball court, or in the office boardroom, the consequence of hiring the wrong person for the job can be catastrophic. An employee's unwillingness to do their own work can create additional work for others; their inability to get along with others can create conflict among their colleagues; and their incapacity to improve upon their own knowledge and skill can affect the long-term growth of the organization. They create a work environment that is contentious, unproductive, and ineffective, which results in an escalating level of stress and resentment as the organization loses its competitive and strategic strengths. Salaries fall, promotional opportunities diminish, and morale suffers—hardly a fun place to work.

Finding the right person is more an art than a science. Even if you do everything right, there is a chance you may still hire the wrong person. What are the attributes of the right person to hire, the one who will help make an organization profitably and yet fun? Generally speaking, I believe there are three. First, they must have the ability to do the job. They must possess the knowledge, skills, education, experience, training, and licenses required of the position. For the most part, these qualifications are the easiest to identify and determine, as you can quantify their education, years of experience, etc.

Second, the person must be someone motivated to do the job, who finds the job interesting, challenging, and responsible. This is more challenging to identify as applicants may not be so forthcoming about the true intent of their ambitions. It may be less about how this job satisfies their career ambitions and more about the need to accept any job. Generally, motivated employees are interested in the job they do and the industry they belong to—their employment history is a great clue to determine someone's motivation. Time and effort should be invested in discovering the passions and desires of the person you are hiring and how your position meets that passion and desire. Ask where they want to go, how this position will help get them there, and how this position will not. These questions illuminate the heart and soul of a person, traits that are far more important in determining who a person really is, rather than the person they are trying to be.

Finally, the right person to hire is someone who would appear manageable once they are on the job. You want someone who is secure, unselfish, and works well with others. This does not mean that they are a conformist or favor consensus over conviction in every situation but that they appear to listen and give credence to differing opinions and viewpoints. Moreover, you should look for someone who is not averse to authority and has a sense of loyalty to a cause that is decent and honorable.

Can you hire the wrong person even if you follow the perfect hiring strategy? It is entirely possible; in fact, if you have not hired the wrong person for the wrong position at some point in your life, you simply have not hired many people. It is inevitable that, at one point, you will hire the wrong person, which is one reason a manager must take the subsequent difficult decision to terminate an employee if and when it is determined that the employee is not able, motivated, or manageable to do the job they were hired to do. An unwillingness or inability of a manager to do so impedes, if not destroys, an organization's ability to survive.

Most employees that I have managed in my career—either directly or through my position in human resources—have had the ability to do the job. Where they have faltered is either their motivation to do their job or their manageability once they were in the job. Where an employee failed, though, it was nearly always their choice to do so. They decided to not show up for work on time, they decided to not complete their assigned projects or tasks, they decided to provide less than helpful service to our customer, and they decided to simply not meet the expectations of their job. In these situations, no matter the skill or ability of a manager, you cannot force an employee to do their job when they have chosen not to do so. As a manager, there are few strategies that you can utilize to assist an employee who continually questions authority, is selfish, is dishonest, refuses to improve upon their own skills or abilities, or has an innate inability to get along with others.

Disciplining an employee is certainly not fun. However, I again believe that most discipline related to employee performance is because an employee chooses not to do their job. Therefore, it should not be a stressful situation for a manager to discipline an employee, as the manager is only responding to the choice of the employee. For the employee would instead choose to meet the stated expectations of the job, discipline is largely circumvented. Though I have disciplined many employees throughout my career, there have been only few occasions that were stressful, mainly because I learned some time ago that the employees put me in the position to discipline them because of choices they made in their own lives.

There is one other reason that disciplining an employee should not be avoided. Employees who choose not to do their job have a tremendous impact on the organization. Their unwillingness to do their job, or to do their job without creating conflict or dissension within their employee ranks, affects the organization's productivity and profitability. So, disciplining the few who cause consternation for the many can be an extraordinary opportunity to make this organization a better, and more fun, place to work.

Several years ago, there was an employee in my previous organization that had considerable skills and abilities and had worked for our company for over twenty years. However, he was extremely negative to our employees, condescending to the customers, and disrespectful to his supervisors. His skills were valuable to the organization, so for a number of years the organization chose to overlook this employee's faults. This was a mistake that greatly affected the culture of the organization.

When I started at that organization, I soon realized that this person had a destructive impact on the organization. Though his skills were valuable, the caustic nature of this person's conduct far outweighed his contributions. This person, in my opinion, needed to change his outlook and demeanor because so many in the organization were affected by his conduct. Not surprising, this person was unwilling to change his basic disposition, mainly because he had been able to act that way without any negative repercussions from the organization.

In this case, the employee was terminated a short while later, and while it caused some dissention in the organization in the short term (when anyone is terminated, there is dissention within the organization mainly because employees wonder who is next), within a few days employees felt the burdens and stresses of working with this individual lifted. Over the course of the next month, morale rose, and you see and feel the mood lighten within that division. Then, when we hired that person's replacement and saw that his skills and abilities were similar to the person who was terminated because of the caustic nature of his personality, the consensus was that people wished the organization had taken that action much earlier.

I believe that, with few exceptions, such employees are a burden to management and are not only self-destructive but destructive to the organization at large. Unless a manager takes strong, affirmative, and often unpopular steps to address the unwillingness of employees to meet the expectations of their position—and thus relieve the stress and conflict inherent with employees who choose not to do their job—it is a herculean task to make work a fun place to be.

AN EXTRAORDINARY ATTITUDE

Your attitude is the outward manifestation of who you are. Those with a bad attitude express negativity and disapproval; those with a positive attitude express exactly the opposite, not only an uplifting, optimistic spirit but a sunny disposition that permeates every thought and every action. They think the best, do the best, and hope for the best in everything they do and everyone they meet. They are magnets for everything that is good, and we strive to be around such people because they make us feel even better about ourselves. They make our life fun.

- Importantly, you decide what your attitude will be—about yourself, your job, your employees, and your organization. The good news is that you can change your attitude, though it is quite difficult. Unfortunately, we have so many experiences that taint our attitude, including various prejudices and biases on age, weight, gender, etc., that we find changing our attitude is a heroic task. In fact, people who have influence in our lives, such as our parents, cousins, teachers, supervisors, coworkers, and friends, pass on some of these negative attitudes through their words and actions, and we tend to mimic those who influence our thoughts and actions.

There are a multitude of other influences affecting your attitude, including self-esteem, self-image, and self-confidence. Why so many fall on the negative side of the attitude scale as opposed to the positive side may be a mystery to some, but I am convinced that everyone can achieve a positive, uplifting attitude. An extraordinary attitude is achieved by overcoming the negative influences in our culture and by seeking the positive influences in our world. These positive influences to an extraordinary attitude would, at a minimum, include:

- First, eat right and get the proper exercise. Improve your self-image, whether that be through clothes, health, or body. It is difficult to think and feel positively unless your mind and body are of the same disposition.

- Second, surround yourself with only the most positive and optimistic influences, whether the television shows you watch, the books that you read, the friends that you choose to spend your time with, or the organization that you choose to work for. There are a number of other, simple tasks that you can follow to better your attitude. Paint your walls a lighter color, plant more trees in your yard so that you see the green of the trees rather than the gray of the concrete, or listen to uplifting music that energizes your soul. For those that live in areas where you can't plant trees or you aren't allowed to paint your walls, don't let that stop you. Create tapestries on your walls with pieces of fabric or find some beautiful indoor plants.

Think of ways to inject comfort, joy, health, peace, and beauty into your life. Noisy neighbor upstairs? Buy a pair of earplugs or portable music with headphones. Can't sleep on an old mattress? Make a nest of comfortable blankets on the floor instead. Don't let the world affect your happiness, and don't take no for an answer. Search for happiness, because happiness begets positivity; so eliminate those influences that draw you down a path of selfishness, dishonesty, and hate, and instead choose the influences that reinforce what you are striving to become.

- Third, take responsibility for your future. Search for the professional and personal life that brings you peace and happiness, and then never deviate from the path that takes you there. Those that are the most happy are those who feel they have something worthwhile to do and to contribute. More importantly, stop blaming others for your failures in life. Even in those situations where you feel least in control of your life, there are still some choices you can make to improve upon your circumstances. You do largely control your own destiny, rather than your destiny being determined by outside influences such as your parents, friends, and coworkers. You must, at some point, accept the fate that you have chosen, and then if you want to change that fate, you must have the courage and fortitude to do so.

- Finally, develop a positive philosophy of life that permeates all you do, and constantly remind yourself of your philosophy. As I mentioned, each and every morning and evening I remind myself to "always look for the good along the road of life." I also remember to "go down swinging for what I believe in." It reminds me of the goodness I seek, of the difference that I can make, and never to compromise on those two beliefs as I travel to reach my destiny. I hope you do the same.

SUMMARY: MAKE WORK FUN

My kids—Gunner and Toria—love roller coasters. I remember the first time we visited the DollyWood Theme Park outside of Knoxville, Tennessee (we've been there twice). My kids rode the Thunderhead rollercoaster twenty-three straight times (I rode it three times and sat out the rest!). Each and every time they rode that rollercoaster they had a look of absolute wonderment and excitement. It was an unbelievable time because it was fun, and they never wanted the fun to stop. I have never forgotten that lesson.

Wouldn't it be great if we could create a workplace that is similar to riding a thrilling rollercoaster each and every day? Wouldn't it be great if we could work for a manager who is positive, upbeat, has an optimistic view of his job and his life, and wants nothing more than to make work fun? Those managers most adept at creating a fun place to work do so because they care about people, have found the right person for the right job within their organization, and have an extraordinary attitude.

Employees want to work for a manager who makes work fun and who helps make an organization a fun place to work. This is the type of manager and the type of person I want to be: someone who enjoys what they do, enjoys who they do it with, and enjoys the journey they have chosen. It is not an impossible feat; it is clearly within everyone's grasp, if only you have the courage to choose your own path in life and then never waiver or falter in the pursuit of those ambitions. Similar to a rollercoaster, it is an opportunity to face a challenge and a chance to give it your best shot. It would make a manager a fun person to work with and an organization a fun place to work. To me, that is fun and, more importantly, it is possible.

Be a Good Person

More than any other trait or attribute, good managers are defined by their ability to be good people. Few college courses, textbooks, managerial theories, corporate training sessions, or business books promote the importance of being a good person in order to be a good manager. The reason is because it is very difficult to not only define what a good person is, but then to train someone to be a good person. In a field dedicated to researching theories to resolve conflict, broaden communication channels, motivate employees to perform, and other similar managerial challenges, the concept of goodness seems too ethereal, too psychological, and too philosophical.

Good, in my opinion, is a thought or a trait that is desirable. Most organizations and employees search for managers who are honest not deceitful, constructive not obstructive, encouraging not discouraging, generous not selfish, and kind-hearted not mean-spirited. They search for these traits because they describe a person who is decent and honorable. A decent person is one who is well-mannered, polite, and unfailingly kind. This person is decent because, no matter how they are treated, they treat others with a sense of dignity and compassion uncommon to most people.

An honorable person is one who is principled and moral. His or her beliefs, aspirations, and integrity are never compromised, no matter the money, power, or fame offered.   Decent and honorable managers undertake their responsibilities with the noblest of intentions and actions; they embody one who is good.

As young adults, we idolize the superstar athlete, the celebrated singer, or the famous movie star. We idolize them because of their phenomenal athletic ability, their soaring voice, or their stunning good looks. Such idolization, though, is fleeting: the superstar athlete eventually loses the big game; the celebrated singer releases a poor selling CD; and beautiful movie star's looks start to fade. The public loses interest in yesterday's hero and replaces tem with the better athlete, the more exciting singer, and the more striking movie star. Fame fades, except for those very few who are respected and admired as much for their famous accomplishments as for the genuine goodness in which they live their life.

NASCAR driver Tony Stewart spends much of his time and money building parks for children; Academy Award winner Audrey Hepburn spent a good part of her life working for the United Nation's Children's fund (UNICEF, which helps children living in poverty in developing countries); and President Jimmy Carter has built hundreds of homes for the poor through the Habitat for Humanity organization. These individuals use every gift and talent they have been given to reach the loftiest of ambitions. These are wealthy and famous individuals, to be sure, and we applaud their accomplishments. But they are respected more for what they have done with their fame and good fortune than for the fame and fortune. They live decent and honorable lives, and recognize the importance of giving back to their fellow man. We are drawn to such individuals because of the basic goodness of their character and strive to emulate their example.

It is this trait of genuine goodness that differentiates a good person from a bad person, a good manager from a bad manager. Regrettably, I believe that this trait is too often missing in a manager. There are those managers consumed with hate, envy, jealously, contempt, and vindictiveness. Such people consumed with evil thoughts perform evil actions; it is all they know. Sadly, in nearly any organization there are those bad managers and bad people that you must work with as supervisors, colleagues, or employees.

I remember only too well my own experience. Over the course of a year, I witnessed this manager systematically destroy a number of careers. In one instance, this manager offered a high-level position to someone from out of state. The candidate accepted, resigned his current position, and moved from that state. Shortly after he began his new position, he was told his services were no longer required. He was unable to return to his previous job, which greatly impacted his ability to provide for his family.

Later that year, this manager inadvertently and inappropriately received confidential information about an applicant for employment in her department. Based on this information, the manager decided not to extend an offer of employment. This action was not only unethical, but illegal, and I conveyed these thoughts to the manager. Needless to say, these thoughts were not received well.

Shortly thereafter, the manager tried to separate me from the organization, using the pretext of a corporate layoff. I notified the organization of the manager's unethical and illegal intention, and an internal investigation began. The investigation revealed the layoff was not consistent with the organization's policies and procedures and, more importantly, that the manager had acted deceptively and dishonestly. The action was reversed, and those in her department were assured that such devious and deceptive actions by this manager would not reoccur.

Our department was fortunate that a courageous person dedicated to fairness appeared and challenged the actions of this manager. Justice was done, with the manager's career ending shortly thereafter. Thankfully, my career recovered, though others were not so lucky, which underscores the vital role of a manager not only in the organization but in regard to an employee's future. Those hired or promoted into a managerial position then have the opportunity make decisions the consequences of which can be highly advantageous or highly destructive, not only to your career, but to your very way of life. For the most part, it is your manager who makes the recommendation or decision on your hiring and subsequent promotions. They have some discretion on the tasks and responsibilities that you are assigned, culminating in an annual evaluation on those assignments. They originate, recommend, and often decide the level of employee discipline.

More importantly, managers are the conduit through which your performance is relayed to other employees and managers. That assessment establishes your reputation among your colleagues and among those who may consider you for future promotion; it also establishes an all-too-often permanent record of your worth in that position and in that organization. For some, this assessment may be inaccurate and unfair and not represent their performance. That reputation is also incredibly difficult to overcome once it is established for three primary reasons. First, you often do not know who is aware of your performance. Managers have greater access to other supervisors and managers than nonmanagers, so their circle of interaction is broader. Second, you are often not aware of the message being conveyed about your performance. It is a challenge when you do not know who to defend yourself to and about what. Finally, people tend to believe at least some of what they hear or see; therefore, initial discussions about your performance form a perception of your overall abilities. Changing this perception is exceedingly difficult because your message contrasts with what they have been told and what they may in fact believe.

These adverse actions can change the very direction and trajectory of your life. With few exceptions, a person's employment salary provides their primary income, which then determines the type of home or apartment they purchase, the neighborhood they live in, the car they drive, the school their children attend, and the social and entertainment opportunities they may pursue (hobbies, health clubs, movies, travel, etc). If the manager making decisions about a person's employment and future employability is not a good person, one with only the noblest of intentions, his or her impact on an employee's career can be irreversible and catastrophic, often with a sense of finality.

Such is the critical importance of working for a good manager who is also a good person. The difficult question, of course, is how a manager becomes a good person. I doubt there will be universal concurrence in the traits of a good person, but I would propose that a good manager—and, by nature, a good person—becomes good because they possess five key traits:

■ First, they are unbelievably kind-hearted. Kindness is not limited to the common courtesies of "hello" and "how are you" but also includes offering encouraging thoughts and a helpful hand even before it is asked.

■ Second, they control the destructive human emotions of ego, jealously, and selfishness. Ego is the inflated image or impression of oneself; jealously is the resentment of the possessions or successes of someone else; and selfishness is placing your own interests before others. A good manager believes they are no better than their subordinates, encourages the successes of their peers, and strives to help others achieve their ambitions (even at the expense of their own).

■ Third, they tell the truth. In nearly any walk of life, it is virtually impossible to overcome a reputation for deceit and duplicity once established. Conversely, honest managers elicit their employees' respect and admiration because they trust their manager's word, never feeling the need to question or scrutinize their manager's action for an ulterior motive or hidden agenda. Employees feel more secure in their job, which helps to create a less stressful work environment.

■ Fourth, they do what's right. What's right is that which improves the human condition, that which improves upon our future. Good people expend the effort and bear the burden to do what's right not necessarily for them but for that which advances our society.

■ Fifth, they always look for the good along the road of life—my personal motto. I believe good people think the best, do the best, and therefore become the best. It starts with an outlook of genuine goodness, and the statement "always look for the good along the road of life," reminds me on a daily basis to keep that outlook in the forefront of my life.

SUMMARY: BE A GOOD PERSON

Of all the attributes of a good manager detailed in this book, the one that is the most difficult to train, learn, and attain is that of good person. A person must have the desire to truly transform his or her character and basic disposition to one of generosity and decency. One who struggles to purge the evils of hate, envy, jealously, and other personal insecurities from their thoughts and actions, and instead strives to live a better life is a rare person indeed.

If a manager making those decisions is good, we have found a person who will call the game fair and honestly, who will reward (or punish) our efforts without malice or hate. We have found someone with our own best interests at heart, and someone who will help—not hinder—our personal and professional ambitions. We have, indeed, found an exceptional employee: a manager who is a good person.

Employees feel they will be treated more fairly by managers with these attributes, which is the reason organization's search for goodness in a person. I believe most employees reward good managers with a level of loyalty, commitment, and effort unsurpassed in an organization. With few exceptions, you tend to work the hardest for those who work hard for you; you tend to do the best for others who do the best for you; you tend to treat those well who treat you well; and, finally, you tend to be decent and honorable to those who are decent and honorable to you.

I also believe an employee can also become a good person because they have had the shining example of a good manager to follow. By example, they can learn to be incredibly kind-hearted, control their most destructive human emotions, tell the truth, do what's right, and always looks for the good along the road of life. Goodness begets goodness; all that is needed is a guide. Hopefully, the lessons in this book start on you on that journey.

The Last Word

As with most professions, the role of a manager has been transformed considerably these past few decades. Our employees, our customers, and our competition have changed as the years progress, so it stands to reason that management must do so as well. We see the demands of the position have increased the hours need to perform those demands and exacerbated the stress in managers' lives as they attempt to balance these escalating work demands with some semblance of a personal life. And then, since 2008, the collapse of the economy has brought doubt to the competence and ethical comportment for those in the managerial profession.

To be sure, it is a difficult time to be a manager, and in such times, those in the profession are looking for a tool or strategy as a guide through the trials and tribulations of their job. And there are thousands of weekly magazine articles, hundreds of books at the neighborhood bookstore, and dozens of courses at the local college all addressing that topic that mystifies much of the organizational world: what makes a good manager. Magnifying the answer to this question is the increasing importance of the role a manager plays in an organization's success, along with the growing complexity for the profession in today's globally competitive environment.

One does not need decades of experience, and a PhD in organizational management, to be a good manager. In reality, there are several basic principles, or attributes, that are common to the most effective manager. It's similar to a baseball player learning how to hold a bat or a golfer choosing the right club for a particular shot. It starts with the fundamentals—the basics. These attributes are simple, and they can be learned by those with the drive and determination to be a better manager and a better person.

This book highlights the six fundamentals of management, six attributes of a good, decent, honorable, and effective manager. The hope is that you adopt these attributes as you manage your employees, your department, your business, and even your life. In summary, these attributes were:

First, that you like what you do. Management is a physically and emotionally draining profession, filled with many challenges and disappointments. The profession may not be for everyone, but if managing employees and an organization is what you like to do, it can also be the most exhilarating experience of your life, allowing you to have a greater role in the development and success of an employee and an organization. There are few professions more rewarding.

Second, knowledge. Managers with the greatest breadth and depth of knowledge simply have a better opportunity to make a more reasoned and intelligent decision on a wide range of organizational issues, from the hiring of an employee to the development of the organization's strategic plan. This knowledge, gained through a broad education and diverse experiences, better prepares a manager to make the right decision, at the right time, and for the right reason.

Third, solid organizational skills. Decades ago, an organization's primary competitor was in the same town or state; rarely was that competitor in another country. Today's globally competitive environment dramatically increased the complexity of the managerial profession, requiring a relentless focus on quality and costs. Organizations are often required to produce more goods at a lower cost, which necessitates that a manager learn the art of planning, delegating, prioritizing, and managing time. These are the basic building blocks of a manager's competence; without this foundation very little in an organization can be accomplished.

Fourth, work hard. The world is replete with talented people who have done little to perfect and utilize their talent. There are superb painters who never market their paintings because they fear criticism; phenomenal writers who do not publish their books because they fear failure. What a shame. Managers may have certain talents—say, for instance, the ability communicate well, or an ability to decipher complex mathematical computation—but unless they have the drive and determination to maximize and market their talents they become a cautionary tale for an unrealized promise and wasted lives.

Fifth, fun. To be honest, several colleagues believe this attribute to be the least important of a manager and have offered several attributes they feel are more important to include in this book. I, however, have stood my ground! I am convinced that people yearn for fun in their life, for a time and place where they feel comfortable and are welcomed regardless of their challenges and difficulties. If that place can be where they work, where their manager instills a sense of adventure and excitement in what they do and who they do it for, I believe the repercussions for such a work environment will lead to a level of loyalty, commitment, and productivity rarely seen in an organization.

Finally, a good person. No matter the attributes you possess as a manager, I believe that your success and failure as a manager rests on your ability to be a good person. A good person is one who lives a decent and honorable life, who is incredibly kind-hearted, controls the most destructive human emotions, tells the truth, does what's right, and always looks for the good along the road of life. As employees search for the perfect job in the perfect career, look for a manager that is first a kind and generous person. As organizations search for the brightest, most driven employees, they should look first for a decent and honorable manager who has only the purest and noblest intentions for the employees. Inevitably, I believe our happiness or unhappiness, success or failure, in the workplace depends on finding that good person. Never settle until you find such a person to work with; never stop until you become one yourself.

The quest for goodness in your personal and professional life is an exhilarating quest, one that is attainable to those with the drive and desire to live a good and decent life. I sincerely hope you are, or will become, that type of manager and that type of person.

Every person is given a platform: a teacher, a singer, or a carpenter.

What you do with that platform determines the pride in your past, the happiness in your present, and the legacy for your future.

References

Long, Huey. Huey Long: The Man, His Mission, and Legacy. Accessed November 15, 2009, at http://www.hueylong.com/life-times/assassination.php

www.ingramcontent.com/pod-product-compliance
Lightning Source LLC
Chambersburg PA
CBHW022100170526
45157CB00004B/1412